Rose Orlando's
SEAFOOD COOKBOOK

Barbour and Company, Inc.
164 Mill Street
Westwood, New Jersey

Dedicated to all of my children:
Terri, Kimberly, Kathleen, Joey, Lisa, and Maureen,
who are not sure that I knew what I was doing "Then
and Now nor Before and After."

Contents

Foreword

This cookbook is borne out of a weekly recipe newsletter I've been writing for my Ft. Myers customers. The newsletter has generated a lot of interest from them, and through it I've been able to share my love of seafood and of cooking with many people. I hope to share that love, and experience, with many, many more.

This is not just a cookbook. It's a part of my life. I've been involved with cooking and preparing food all my life. It just seems to come naturally. I love to experiment in the kitchen. I don't think I ever make a recipe the same way twice. That's why I offer variations with many of them in this book. I've also included several Italian-seafood recipes. Italian was my first food-love, and these recipes are from those days, simply converted to seafood.

Seafood is smart eating. Fish and shellfish are excellent sources of high-quality protein, many valuable minerals, and essential A, B-complex, and D vitamins. An average serving of seafood has less than 200 calories; some of the leaner varieties, such as flounder, as few as 80. Fish is also very low in sodium (it's good for low-sodium diets) and fat, the fats being mainly polyunsaturated, which is becoming increasingly important to health-conscious people.

Besides being delicious and nutritious, most seafood is fast and easy to prepare. I hope that you find many recipes in this book that you'll use over and over, and that you enjoy them as much as I have enjoyed sharing them with you.

Rose Orlando

Fish

How to Cook Perfect Fish

The Canadian Theory: This is the basic rule for all fish and works with baking, broiling, frying, and grilling. Cook fish for 10 minutes per inch of thickness. This applies for fillets, steaks, whole fish, stuffed or not—measure the thickest part. And the temperature has to be high, 400-450 degrees.

Baking: Bake fish according to the above rule in a preheated 400-450 degree oven. Bake it uncovered and basted with butter or sauces. There are several good sauces for baking fish in this book.

Broiling: Broil pieces less than an inch thick 2-4 inches from the heat, thicker pieces 5-6 inches away. The Canadian Theory applies to the whole fish; broil each side for half the total time. Very thin fillets don't need to be turned.

Charcoal Grilling: Both the fish and the grill should be oiled, and the grill preheated. Baste fish several times while grilling. For a smoky flavor, add water-soaked hardwood chips to the coals.

Pan-frying: Heat a quarter-inch of oil in the pan till it's very hot but not smoking, and fry fish according to the 10-minute-per-inch rule; again, each side for half the total time.

Deep-frying: Heat enough oil to submerge breaded or battered fish to 375 degrees. Cook the fish according to thickness, as above. Drain them on paper towels. Be sure the oil returns to 375 degrees before frying more fish.

Poaching: Boil enough water, wine, or court bouillon to submerge fish. Add the fish, bring the liquid to a boil again, then reduce the heat to a simmer and time your fish from this point.

Basting: Brush fish with oil, melted butter, wine, or marinade. (see "Sauces").

Breading: Dip fish in a mixture of egg beaten with a little milk, then lightly coat the fish with a mixture of one part flour to three parts cornmeal, and refrigerate the coated pieces for about 20 minutes.

Batter: Mix one cup of dry pancake mix with one cup of beer, club soda, or sparkling cider, and beat this till it's smooth. Dip fish into this batter and coat the pieces evenly, letting the excess drain off.

Foil pouch: Measure the thickness of the pouch and subtract an inch, or 10 minutes, from this figure. *For example:* If the pouch is 3 inches thick, cook it for 20 minutes. An oiled paper bag works the same way, but you'll need a lower heat—no more than 375 degrees. (I'm sure you don't want to serve "Flaming Paper Bag of Fish.")

Cooking with wine: Several recipes in this book use wine. The basic thing to remember is when alcohol is heated, the alcohol dissipates and all that's left is a flavor. If ya don't like to use wine, though, white grape juice will substitute. Use twice the grape juice that is called for in the recipe (for wine) and boil it down to half its original volume. The darker grape juices work, but they discolor seafoods. There are many non-alcoholic wines and champagnes on the market that work well also. Just use the white, blush or pinks.

Cooking in a microwave: Most of the recipes in this book can be converted to the microwave. Here, though, the Canadian rule doesn't apply. Along with the following guidelines, your best bet is to use your microwave manual.

Cook fish covered, with a lid or plastic wrap, on high. Use less liquid than in oven-baking, and less cooking time —how much depends on your microwave. Always place the thickest parts of the fish toward the outside of the dish. Fish are done when they flake in the center; test them with a fork.

And most important, fish don't have to be browned to be "done." Overcooking fish is as bad as overcooking steak. Whatever cooking method you use, fish is done when it has become opaque or white (no longer translucent) and when it flakes with a fork.

White Fish

Buttermilk Fried Fish

Serves 2-3

- 1 **lb. fish fillets, boneless no matter what species**
- 1 **Tbs. lemon juice**
- 1 **cup buttermilk**

Rinse and pat-dry the fillets, cut in small pieces or standard size, whichever suits you. Mix the lemon juice and buttermilk and add the fish, making sure to immerse in the liquid. Cover and refrigerate for about an hour.

Mix the following in a shallow dish or pie plate:

- 1 **cup all-purpose flour**
- ½ **cup yellow cornmeal**
- 1 **tsp. salt, or pepper to taste**
- 1 **tsp. white pepper**
- 1 **tsp. paprika**

Remove the fish from the refrigerator, one piece at a time, and let the excess liquid drip off into the bowl. Coat the fish with the cornmeal-flour mixture. Lay the breaded pieces on a rack, and set the rack on a cookie sheet. Then refrigerate the rack of fish for another hour.

Heat about a quarter-inch of cooking oil, or whatever you prefer, in a skillet on medium heat, and fry the fish without crowding them. If the fillets are thin, they will take only 3 minutes for each side. Cook until the fish flakes with a fork and has turned opaque. The "10 minutes per inch thickness" applies here. If the pieces are 1 inch thick cook 5 minutes on each side.

The second time in the refrigerator is important. This gives the coating time to dry and cling to the fish. This may seem like a long drawn-out affair, but it's worth every bit of time that you spend on it.

You can also deep-fry this fish. You won't even need tartar sauce, it's so good just plain. You can substitute sesame seeds or pecans (ground or finely chopped) for the cornmeal.

Herb-Mustard Fish Fillets

Serves 3-5

- 1½   lbs. any fish fillets
- ¼   cup dry white wine
- ⅓   cup salad oil
- ¼   cup white-wine vinegar
- 1   Tbs. minced onion
- 1   tsp. Italian herbs
- 1   garlic clove, crushed and minced
- ¼   cup spicy brown mustard

Rinse and pat-dry the fillets that you have cut into serving-size pieces.

Mix all other ingredients. Add the fish fillets, and turn to coat, then cover this with plastic film and refrigerate for 2 to 4 hours.

When you're ready to cook, preheat the oven and lay the fillets out in a single layer on a well buttered baking pan or dish. Bake them at 425 degrees, or broil them 3 or 4 inches from the heat. Either way 10 minutes per inch.

You can try all types of mustard with this recipe, Dijon, plain, or whatever. I use the white-wine vinegar because the red-wine vinegar darkens the fish. A regular white vinegar works fine too, not all of us stock white-wine vinegar.

I used a wire basket for a grill with this recipe and it was excellent.

7

Italian-Style Baked Fish

Serves 4 to 6

    1 Tbs. dried rosemary or 2 Tbs. fresh
    ¼ cup dry white wine
    4 Tbs. butter or margarine, melted or olive oil
    1 Tbs. freshly minced garlic
    2 lbs. uniformly sized fish fillets
         (1 inch or more is best)
  Salt and pepper

Preheat the oven to 350 degrees.

Pulverize the rosemary in a blender. Pour the wine and butter into the blender and briefly mix with the rosemary. Then stir in the garlic.

Place the fillets in a buttered shallow pan with space between each, pour the blender mixture over the fish, and sprinkle them with salt and pepper.

Bake 10 minutes per inch or till the fish flakes. This may take a little longer than usual because the temperature is not as high as the 10-minute theory calls for. You can use 400 degrees if you like, but this is one dish I like cooked a little slower. You can also baste the fish about halfway through.

You don't have to pulverize the rosemary. I do because I don't care for the brittleness of whole rosemary. But I love the flavor.

Sesame Seed Baked Fish

Serves 4 (½ lb. per person)
- 2 lbs. white fish fillets
- ¼ cup seasoned or plain bread crumbs
- ¼ cup grated Parmesan cheese
- ¼ cup sesame seeds
- 1 egg beaten slightly with 1 Tbs. water or milk
- 3 Tbs. melted butter or margarine or sesame seed oil

Mix the bread crumbs, Parmesan cheese, and sesame seeds on a pie plate. Preheat the oven to 375 degrees. Butter or oil a pan large enough for the fish fillets to fit into.

Dip the fish into the egg wash, letting the excess drain off, then coat the fillets in the crumb, cheese, and seed mixture, patting well, and lay them into the oiled pan. Drizzle butter or oil over the fillets, and bake at 10 minutes per inch. Fish are done when they turn white or opaque and when they flake easily. There is no need to add salt. You'll never miss it.

I like the flavor of nuts or anything crunchy added to my fish, of any kind. I especially like sesame seeds. I bake or broil a fish fillet very simply with butter, lemon, salt and pepper. When it's ready to serve, I sprinkle some toasted sesame seeds on top. Easy, and oh, so good! Or I heat sesame seeds in a skillet on medium heat, shaking the skillet to keep the seeds moving around. I use a dry skillet, no oil or fat of any kind! This takes a few minutes.

If you're watching your intake of fat and oils, you can bake or microwave the fillets with lemon and add the toasted sesame seeds when you're ready to serve.

Broiled Fish Fillets with Mayonnaise

Serves 2-3

    1 lb. white fillets
    ½ cup mayonnaise (*not* salad dressing)
    1 tsp. white pepper
 2–3 dashes aromatic bitters

Rinse the fillets and dry them on paper towels. Mix the mayonnaise, white pepper, and aromatic bitters and this mixture over the fish, coating each fillet entirely.

Broil them 3–4 inches from the heat on an oiled broiler rack for ten minutes per inch. If the fillets are quite thin, don't try to turn them.

This is excellent with any kind of fish, swordfish, halibut, mackerel, dolphin, tuna—anything you can get on the hook. The mayonnaise keeps the fish moist and gives it a delicate flavor.

If you don't have aromatic bitters on hand, substitute lemon juice.

Broiled Coconut-Coated Fish Fillets

Serves 2-4

    ½ cup prepared baking mix
    ½ cup flake coconut
     Salt and pepper
    ½ cup heavy whipping cream
    2 Tbs. spicy-brown mustard
    1 lb. white fish fillets
    4 Tbs. butter or margarine

Combine the baking mix, coconut, salt, and pepper in a shallow dish.

Mix the cream and mustard in a medium size bowl and immerse the fillets in this, then refrigerate it for about half an hour.

Remove the fillets, draining excess batter from them, and coat them in the above dry mixture. Broil them on a lightly oiled rack of a broiler pan, with melted butter drizzled over them, for about three minutes on each side.

This recipe is best with thick fillets. The thin ones can't stand up to the turning.

I serve this with a bottle of sweet-and-sour sauce, no extra work. Just warm it slightly. I have also tried a hot Chinese mustard in place of the spicy brown, and it's very good. You know your own family's tastes for that, though.

Broiled Fish with
Orange Sauce & Sesame Seeds

I put this recipe together to get my daughter to eat fish. It worked!

Serves 2-4

    1 lb. white fish fillets
    ¼ cup orange juice
    2 Tbs. catsup
    2 Tbs. oil
    1 Tbs. soy or teriyaki sauce
    1 Tbs. lemon juice
  2-3 Tbs. sesame seeds
    Pepper

In a bowl, combine the orange juice, catsup, cooking oil,

soy or teriyaki sauce, lemon juice, and pepper. Pour this over the fish fillets in a shallow dish. Cover and refrigerate it for about 2 hours.

Drain the fish, reserving the marinade, and cook in a greased shallow pan about 4 inches from the heat. Use the 10-minute-per-inch guide. Baste them once with the marinade, which should be heated just to boiling.

Sprinkle this with sesame seeds before serving. You can also pour more marinade over the fish on the serving plate.

I don't add any salt to the marinade or the fish, because there's enough in the catsup and the soy sauce.

Fish Poached in Saffron Milk

Serves 4-6

- **1 cup whole milk**
- **2 Tbs. butter or margarine**
- **½ tsp. ground saffron or threads**
- **Salt and pepper**
- **2 lbs. white fish fillets**
- **1 Tbs. each butter or margarine and flour**

Heat the milk, butter, and seasoning in a covered saucepan, slowly, just to simmering. Add the fillets and let this simmer till the fish flakes with a fork, then carefully remove them with a spatula and lay them on a warmed platter.

Melt the tablespoon of butter and mix it with the flour. Add this to the hot-milk mixture and stir well till it's slightly thickened. Pour this over the fish and sprinkle it with freshly chopped parsley.

I've used smoked fish in the same way, and it's delicious. This dish is great with small potatoes cooked by themselves and then added to the milk sauce. Served with a green vegetable such as broccoli, it makes a great, nutritious meal.

Halibut, Sole, and Flounder (diet)

Halibut or Swordfish Steaks with Tomato and Basil Sauce

Serves 4–6

- 1 lb. fresh plum tomatoes
- ½ cup fresh basil leaves
- 2 Tbs. white-wine vinegar
- 1 Tbs. capers, rinsed and drained
- Salt and pepper
- 2 lb. fresh halibut or swordfish steaks, frozen or thawed

Peel, seed, and chop the tomatoes. Chop the basil leaves finely. Combine the two and allow them to marinate at room temperature for about 2 hours, or overnight in the refrigerator.

Blend the vinegar, capers, salt, and pepper into the tomato-basil mixture.

Brush the steaks with butter or margarine and broil them at 10 minutes per inch. Remove the fish from the broiler, cover with the sauce and slide back into the broiler just long enough to heat the sauce through.

This makes a perfect light dish. The tomato sauce covers the fish without making it too mushy–so long as you don't overcook it. And there's no fat in the sauce, no fat at all if you coat the fish with a vegetable spray instead of butter. And, of course, you control the amount of salt.

Halibut with Creamy Hollandaise Sauce

Serves 4-6

2	lbs. fresh halibut	1 or 2	dashes hot sauce
2	cups boiling water	½	cup milk
1	tsp. salt	½	cup water
1	small onion	2	egg yolks
1 or 2	bay leaves	2	Tbs. lemon juice
½	cup butter	½	tsp. grated
2	tsp. flour		lemon rind
¼	tsp. salt	2	Tbs. capers

Put the fish in a baking pan, then add the other ingredients, and bake this at 400 degrees for 15-20 minutes, or till the fish flakes. Keep this warm.

Melt the butter in a saucepan, and blend in the flour, salt, and hot sauce. Then add the milk and water and cook this while stirring till it's smooth and thick.

Add a small amount of this hot mixture to the beaten egg yolks and beat this well. Then return this to the rest of the hot mixture and cook it for 1 minute. Stir in the lemon juice, lemon rind, and drained capers and spoon this sauce over the halibut.

Sole Rollups

Serves 4

8 thin sole fillets (the thinnest ya can find)
one 8-oz. pkg. cream cheese, room temperature
4 green onions, thinly sliced, including some
    green tops
1 garlic clove, crushed and minced to a paste

Rinse the fillets and pat them very dry. Mix the cheese, onions, and garlic until they're well-blended. Spread a small amount of the cheese mixture on each fillet. Leave it thicker in the center. Don't spread too close to the edges; it will all melt and run into the pan.

Roll up the fillets very loosely and gently, place them seam-side down in a buttered casserole pan or dish, drizzle melted butter over them, and bake at 350 degrees till they're done.

Sometimes the cream will run out the sides, but if you're very gentle with the rolling, they should be OK. After rolling the fillet, gently squeeze the outside edges together. This helps hold in the filling.

Stuffed Rolled-Flounder

Serves 4

Four 8-oz. flounder, sole, grouper or any thin, white
  lean fish fillets
2 Tbs. butter or margarine
Enough flour for coating rollups

Stuffing:

¼ cup minced onion
1 garlic clove, minced
2½ Tbs. butter or margarine
½ cup bread crumbs
¼ cup black olives, pitted and chopped
one 1-oz. tin anchovies, drained and minced, or
  anchovy paste
¼ tsp. sage, rubbed
Salt and pepper

Sauté the onion and garlic in the butter or margarine. Put the sautéed onion and garlic in a bowl and add the bread crumbs, olives, anchovies, sage, salt, and pepper, and mix well.

Lay out the fillets, cut-side up, and divide the stuffing among them. Don't spread the stuffing too close to the edges. Roll them up and fasten them with toothpicks, then dust them in the flour, and place them seam-side down in hot melted butter in a large skillet, and lightly brown them on all surfaces.

Transfer the rollups to a baking dish, spread with cashew butter, and bake at 350 degrees till the fish flakes.

Cashew Butter:

- ½ cup butter or margarine
- ¼ cup minced cashews

Beat the butter and cashews in a mixing bowl till light and fluffy. It's excellent!

Shrimp Rollups

Serves 4-5. Makes 12 small, thin fillets

- ¼ lb. small shrimp, cooked, peeled, deveined, and finely chopped
- 2 cups fresh bread crumbs
- 1 Tbs. Parmesan or Romano cheese, freshly grated
- 1 Tbs. capers
- 12 medium-size stuffed green olives, minced
- 1 Tsp. dried parsley
- 2 Tbs. tomato sauce
- Salt and freshly ground pepper
- 8 Tbs. unsalted butter, melted
- 1 lb. thin fillets, flounder or sole

Mix all these ingredients together and spread on thin fillets. Don't spread all the way to the edges. The fish should be patted dry with paper towels so the filling will stick. Roll the fillets up, securing them with toothpicks, lay them with the open end down in a buttered pan, leaving little space between each, and bake them at 400 degrees till they're flaky.

Salmon

Salmon Mousse

Serves Buffet of 20 or more
1½ lbs. fresh salmon fillets or steaks

Poach the salmon in a liquid consisting of equal amounts of dry wine and water, add small amounts of parsley, carrots, crushed garlic, onion, black peppercorns, and whatever other seasonings you like, with just a little salt, and bring this wine mixture to a boil. Add the salmon, reduce the heat, cover it tightly, and let this simmer till the salmon flakes easily, or use the 10-minutes-per-inch theory. Strain the salmon, reserve the liquid, then remove the skin and bones and set the salmon aside.

2 envelopes unflavored gelatin
1 tsp. sugar
1¼ cups mayonnaise (*not* salad dressing)
2 Tbs. tomato paste
2 Tbs. fresh lemon juice
2–3 dashes Worcestershire sauce
Salt and pepper

(continued next page)

> **2 hard-boiled eggs, chopped**
> **2 Tbs. freeze-dried chives or fresh dried green-**
>   **onion tops, minced**
> **¼ cup chopped pimiento, well-drained**
> **½ cup heavy whipping cream, whipped**

Pour 1 cup of the above poaching liquid in a small saucepan and sprinkle in the gelatin and sugar, and heat this till the gelatin dissolves.

In another pan, combine the mayonnaise, tomato paste, lemon juice, Worcestershire sauce, salt, and pepper. Stir in the gelatin mixture and chill till it's partially set.

Fold in the salmon, chopped eggs, chives, and chopped pimiento, then fold the whipped cream into this mixture.

Oil a 5-to 7-inch cup fish mold, gently press the mousse into it and chill this till it's firm. If you don't have a fish mold, any bowl or mold that holds at least 6 cups will do.

When it's chilled, dip the mold quickly into hot water to loosen the mousse, and turn it upside down on a lettuce-lined platter. Use either thinly sliced red radishes or cucumbers for "fish scales." Either one makes a nice-looking centerpiece. You can add minced dill or dry dillweed to the mousse if you like.

Serve this with crackers, vegetable sticks, or cocktail rye bread.

Salmon Steaks with Anchovy-Lemon Butter

Serves 2

- 2 salmon steaks (1-1½ inch thick)
- one 1-oz. can flat anchovies
- 2 Tbs. butter
- 1 or 2 Tbs. lemon juice
- ¼ tsp. pepper
- ¼ cup minced parsley

Place the salmon steaks on a heatproof platter or in a shallow baking dish. Place this on a rack in a wok over simmering water, cover the wok and steam the steaks for 15 minutes or till they flake easily when touched with a fork.

While the fish steams mash the anchovies to a paste by gradually adding oil they're packed in. Then add butter and beat till it's smooth. Beat in lemon juice and pepper (add more lemon juice if you need to, for a smooth paste).

Spread some of this mixture over the fish. Sprinkle with minced parsley and garnish with lemon wedges. Serve the remaining sauce separately.

Cold Poached Salmon with Cucumber-Yogurt and Dill

Serves 6

Court Bouillon for Poaching:

- 1½ cups water
- 1 cup white wine
- 1 cup wine vinegar
- 1 small onion, thinly sliced
- 1 small carrot, thinly sliced
- 1 stalk celery, thinly sliced
- 1 bay leaf
- 4–3 parsley sprigs
- Salt

Combine all these ingredients and bring them to a boil, then let them simmer for half an hour.

6 salmon steaks 1–1½ inches thick

Turn the heat up again under the bouillon and salmon steaks. As soon as this returns to a boil, reduce the heat to a low simmer, actually, to a shimmer, and cook this till the salmon flakes.

When they're finished cooking, remove the steaks from the liquid, drain them well and, when cool, wrap them in plastic wrap and refrigerate them till they're cold. This can be done the night before.

Sauce *(Continued next page)*

Dill Sauce *(Continued from previous page)*

1   cup cucumber, finely seeded and
      chopped
½   cup fresh dill weed or 2 Tbs. dried dill
¼   cup white-wine vinegar
1   Tbs. brown sugar
1   Tbs. white sugar
1   cup plain yogurt

Mix all these ingredients in a glass bowl. This makes about two and one-quarter cups. Place the steaks on individual platters, spoon the sauce over each, and garnish them with sprigs of fresh dill or parsley, lemon slices, cold sliced tomatoes or cherry tomatoes, watercress, or hard-boiled egg.

Grouper

Cioppino

Serves 6-8

1 lb. fresh grouper	½ lb. fresh mushrooms, sliced
1 cooked lobster, about 1½ lbs	1 medium-size green or sweet red pepper, sliced
1½ dozen littleneck clams, scrubbed well	3 ripe tomatoes, peeled, seeded, and chopped
1 lb. mussels, scrubbed and debearded	¼ cup tomato paste
3 cups red wine	Salt and pepper
½ cup olive oil	1–2 Tsp. dried basil
½ cup chopped onion	1 lb. medium shrimp, peeled, deveined, and tails removed
2 garlic cloves, chopped	
¼ cup chopped parsley	

Cut the fish into serving-size pieces, about 2-inch squares. Split and clean the lobster. Crack the claws and cut the body and tail into small serving-size pieces. Set the fish and lobster aside.

Steam the clams and mussels in a deep pot with 1 cup of the wine until they open, discard any that haven't opened. Remove them from the broth with a slotted spoon and set them aside. Measure 1 cup of the broth, strain it through a cheesecloth, and set it aside. This broth will appear dark and cloudy but it will clear up later.

Heat the olive oil in a 8-quart soup pot and cook the onion, garlic, parsley, mushrooms, and pepper till the onions are translucent. Add the tomatoes and cook this for 5 minutes. Add the strained broth, the tomato paste, and the remaining 2 cups of wine. Season it with salt and pepper and bring it to a simmer. Then cover the pot, lower the flame, and let it simmer gently for about 20 minutes.

Add the basil and the fish, and let it simmer for about 8 more minutes, or till the fish flakes.

Add the shrimp, clams, mussels, and lobster, and continue cooking at a gentle simmer, covered, till the shrimp are pink.

You'll want to serve this with a good fresh garlic bread –to soak up all the juices!

Grouper Parmesan

Serves 4-6

2 lbs. grouper fillets	1 Tbs. grated onion
1 cup sour cream	Dash hot sauce
¼ cup grated	Salt
Parmesan cheese	Paprika
1 Tbs. lemon juice	Chopped parsley

Cut the grouper into serving-size pieces and lay them in a single layer in a well-buttered baking dish.

Combine the sour cream, cheese, lemon juice, onion, hot sauce, and salt, and spread this over the grouper. Sprinkle this with paprika and bake at 400 degrees till the fish flakes. Garnish it with parsley and serve with lemon wedges.

This recipe can also be prepared in the microwave. And, as in many of the recipes in this book, you can substitute any lean white fish for the grouper.

Grouper Almondine

Serves 4-6

> 2 lbs. grouper fillets
> About 1 cup flour
> Salt and pepper
> 8 Tbs. butter or margarine
> 2 ounces sliced almonds, toasted
> ¼ cup lemon juice
> 2 Tbs. fresh parsley, chopped

Rinse and pat-dry the fillets and cut them into serving-size pieces. Coat them in the flour, salt, and pepper, lay them on a plate in single layers, and refrigerate them till they're ready to cook.

Heat half the butter in a skillet. Remove the fillets from the refrigerator and dust them lightly again with the flour mixture, shaking off any excess. Quickly fry the fish for about 4 minutes on each side or till it flakes or is opaque. Remove the fish.

Add the rest of the butter to the skillet and stir till it's bubbly. Add the almonds, sauté them until light golden brown. Add the lemon juice and cook while stirring till most of the lemon juice is evaporated. Add the parsley and spoon this almond-butter sauce over the fish.

Again, you can substitute any lean white fish for the grouper. This is a fast dish to prepare. And so good!

Spanish-Style Grouper

Serves about 6

       1 cup packaged Paella rice
   1½ lbs. grouper fillets
       Salt and pepper
       2 Tbs. butter or margarine
   one 16-oz. can stewed tomatoes, diced
   one 8-oz. jar marinated artichoke hearts, quartered
       ½ cup stuffed green olives, sliced
       ¼ cup pitted black olives, sliced
       1 tsp. Worcestershire sauce
       3 Tbs. capers

Cook the rice according to the package directions. Cut the fish into 1-inch cubes, add salt and pepper to taste and sauté in butter till it's opaque through. Set this aside and keep warm.

To cook the rice, add the tomatoes, artichoke hearts, olives, Worcestershire sauce and capers. Toss this well and reheat but don't cook it. Add the grouper, toss gently, and reheat it again for about 3 minutes.

This is one of those recipes that I had to make up in a hurry. Some friends called and said their parents were in town and they would like to see me before they left. And I said come over for a quick dinner. I didn't have time to thaw steaks for the grill, but I had some grouper that I bought that afternoon for our own dinner. Thank heavens for canned and dried goods I had in my cabinets! The recipe above is the result. They loved it.

You can serve this with a salad and a good crusty bread, and still have room for dessert and coffee.

Hunter-Style Grouper

Serves 6-8

1½ lbs. grouper fillets, the thickest you can get
2—4 Tbs. butter or margarine
    Salt and pepper

Preheat the broiler. Put the grouper in a baking pan and drizzle butter over it. Sprinkle it with salt and pepper and broil at 10 minutes per inch.

    Butter for pan
 ½ cup onions, sliced
 1 cup fresh mushrooms, sliced
1—2 garlic cloves, minced
 3 Tbs. flour
    Salt and pepper
 1 cup dry white wine
 1 cup chicken broth, or ½ cup clam juice plus
        ½ cup water
 1 cup tomatoes, peeled, seeded, and diced
 ¼ cup fresh parsley, minced
    Hot, cooked rice or noodles

In a skillet cook the butter, onion, mushrooms, and garlic till the onion is tender. Stir in the flour, salt, and pepper, and mix these well. Add the wine, chicken broth or clam juice, and tomatoes, mix this well and cook while stirring on medium-high heat till the mixture is thick and bubbly.

Pour the vegetable sauce over the broiled fish and bake this uncovered at 400 degrees for about 10 minutes and till hot and bubbly all the way through. Sprinkle it with the parsley and serve it with the rice or noodles.

Grouper Casserole with Feta Cheese

Serves 6

- 1 lb. grouper fillets, cut into cubes
- one 16-oz. can French-cut green beans, well-drained
- 3 cups cooked white rice
- ½ cup fresh onion, minced
- 2 cups fresh tomatoes, peeled, seeded, and chopped
- ½ tsp. each, basil and oregano leaves
- ½ cup sliced olives
- ½ cup Feta cheese, cubed and patted dry
- ½ cup bread crumbs
- 2 Tbs. melted butter or margarine

Mix all these ingredients except the bread crumbs and melted butter, and pour them into a buttered 2-quart casserole. Cover this and bake for 20–25 minutes.

After it has baked, sprinkle it with the bread crumbs and melted butter, then return this to the oven and bake it for another 5 or 10 minutes. The fish should flake when pierced with a fork, and the bread crumbs should be a light golden brown.

If your casserole seems just a little dry before baking, drizzle some extra melted butter or margarine over it. Or you can do this at the end of the first 20 minutes in the oven.

I have tried several kinds of fish with this casserole, and though each varies a little, it's always very good.

Grouper Delight

- ½ cup slivered almonds, toasted
- 2 lbs. grouper fillets
- 2 Tbs. butter or margarine, melted

Salt and pepper

- 1 pkg. Hollandaise sauce mix
- 1 small can unsweetened pineapple juice
- ½ cup light brown sugar
- 2 bananas, sliced

Bake the almonds in a shallow pan at 400 degrees for about 3 minutes, then stir them once and continue baking till they're a light golden brown.

Broil the fillets according to their thickness and 4 inches from the heat, sprinkle with melted butter, salt and pepper. Be sure to tuck the thin parts (such as the tail) under the other, thicher parts, so there are no dry, overcooked areas. These are done when they flake and are opaque.

While the fish is broiling, prepare the Hollandaise mix according to the directions, but replace half the liquid called for with pineapple juice.

When the fillets are done, sprinkle them with the brown sugar and bananas, pour the Hollandaise sauce on them, and sprinkle them with the toasted almonds. Now broil these again till they're heated through, 3–5 minutes.

Golden Curried Grouper

Serves 4

 four 8-oz. grouper fillets
   2 Tbs. butter or margarine
2–3 Tbs. honey
   2 Tbs. Dijon mustard
   1 Tbs. prepared mustard
   1 small garlic clove, crushed
   1 tsp. lemon juice
   1 tsp. curry powder
  Salt and pepper

Preheat the oven to 350 degres and arrange the fillets in a buttered shallow pan.

Melt the butter in a saucepan on medium heat. Add the rest of the ingredients and whisk till smooth.

Pour this mixture over the fillets and bake for 10–12 minutes, depending on the thickness of the fillets. You can baste this after 5 minutes, if you like, but it's not necessary.

Lemon Grouper Piccata

Makes 2 large or 4 small servings

  ⅔ cup all-purpose flour
  1 tsp. salt
  ½ tsp. pepper
  ¼ tsp. garlic powder
  1 lb. fresh grouper fillets
5½ Tbs. butter or margarine
  4 Tbs. lemon juice
  2 Tbs. parsley, chopped

Combine the flour, salt, pepper, and garlic powder, and set this aside. Rinse and pat-dry the fillets and remove the bones before cooking. (Or ask your friendly fish man to do it for you.) Dredge the fillets in the flour mixture.

Melt the butter in a large skillet on medium heat and cook the fillets for 4 or 5 minutes on each side, or till they're light golden brown. Drain on paper towels and place them on a preheated platter to keep warm.

Add the lemon juice to the skillet, cook till it comes to a bubble, then add the parsley, spoon this mixture over the fillets and garnish them with lemon slices.

Grouper with Nutty Butter

Serves 2-3
- 1 **lb. grouper fillets**
- **Salt and pepper**
- ¼ **cup hazelnuts, finely ground**
- 2 **Tbs. butter**
- 2 **tsp. cider vinegar**

Rinse and pat-dry the fillets and lay them in a buttered pan so they don't touch. Sprinkle them with salt and pepper and broil them for 10 minutes per inch or until they flake easily.

In the meantime, heat the ground nuts and butter in a small, heavy pan until the butter melts. Remove this from the heat, and stir in the vinegar, and season to taste with salt and pepper.

Pour this hot nutty-butter over the fillets and garnish them with lemon slices and parsley.

Cream-Sauced Avocados with Grouper

Serves 4

2 lbs. grouper fillets
1 cup flour
1 tsp. each salt and
   white pepper
3 Tbs. butter or
   margarine
3 Tbs. court bouillon
   (fish broth) or
   bottled clam
   juice

1 cup whipping
   cream
1 Tbs. sherry
3 small avocados
   or 2 large
Dash of hot sauce
   (optional)

Rinse and pat-dry the fillets and cut them into serving-size pieces of about 8 ounces each. Mix the flour, salt and white pepper on a pie plate and lightly coat the fillets with this. Melt the butter or margarine in a skillet and sauté the fillets till they're light golden brown. When they're done keep them in a warm oven.

Sprinkle a tablespoon of the flour mixture into the skillet. Add the fish broth or clam juice, and the whipping cream and stir this with a wooden spoon, scraping up all the little pieces from the bottom. Cook this over a low heat till the sauce is thick and smooth, then add the sherry.

Slice the avocados into wedges and add these to the sauce. Heat this gently, spooning the sauce over the avocados.

Lay the avocado wedges beside the fillets on individual warmed serving plates and pour the cream sauce over them. Use the extra sauce at the table. Garnish the dish with freshly minced parsley or chives.

I have tried chicken broth in place of the fish broth or clam juice, and it works out just fine. Fish bouillon cubes also substitute. For such a small amount, use whatever you have on hand.

And in case you're worried about all the butter and cream in this dish here's something that might make you feel better: avocados are rich in vitamins and minerals and are thought to lower cholesterol levels in the blood. Just as fish oils are thought to. So go ahead! Enjoy this fantastic combination.

Shad

Long-Time-Baked Shad

Serves 4-6

one	2-lb dressed shad	½	cup chopped onion
½	cup chopped celery	3-4	parsley sprigs
3 or 4	bay leaves	1	cup white wine
1	small whole carrot	3-4	cups hot water
	Salt and pepper		
1	whole lemon, thickly sliced		

Wash and dry the dressed shad. Place the celery, bay leaves, and carrot in the bottom of a fish poacher. Put the rack in next. Lay the shad on the rack, salt and pepper the cavity, and lay the lemon slices in the cavity. Sprinkle the chopped onions over the outside of the fish, allowing some of the pieces to fall to the bottom of the poacher, and lay the parsley springs across the top of the fish.

Pour the cup of wine into the bottom of the poacher. Add just enough water to come to the bottom of the rack but not touching the fish, and cover the poacher tightly with a lid. If the lid doesn't fit tightly, seal the poacher with foil and then add the lid.

Bake the whole poacher at 300 degrees for a least 6 hours. Baste the fish after about 3 hours. Do this very quickly, so as not to lose cooking time.

A friend and ex-boss of mine once told me what to do with a shad after you removed the roe; (Garland loves the roe): Wash and dry the shad, cover it with salt and pepper and lay it out on an oiled oak plank. Then carry it high above your head and go directly to the back door and throw the whole thing into the dumpster!

But, seriously, this is a good fish if done properly. I have to admit to having had help with putting the above recipe together the first time. Colonel Jim and his wife, Suse, have been everywhere. He's retired now. Suse is the first person to introduce me to baked or steamed shad above. This method of cooking disintegrates the small bones of the fish. It is cooked so that the backbone becomes edible too. It's delicious. And cold it makes a great fish salad.

Sautéed Shad Roe with Sherry Sauce

Serves 4

6 Tbs. olive oil	2 Tbs. parsley,
1 cup minced onion	chopped
1 tsp. garlic, minced	2 pairs shad roe
1 large bay leaf	Salt and pepper
2 Tbs. flour	½ cup dry sherry
½ cup canned	
chicken stock	

In a large, heavy skillet, heat 4 tablespoons of the olive oil on medium heat till a light haze forms above the oil. Add the onions, garlic, and bay leaf, and cook this for about 5 minutes, stirring frequently, but don't brown. Add the flour and mix it thoroughly. Pour in the chicken stock and cook on high while stirring till the mixture thickens heavily and comes to a boil. Add the parsley, reduce the heat to low, and let this simmer for about 3 minutes.

Heat the remaining 2 tablespoons of olive oil in a large, heavy skillet. Sprinkle the roe with salt and pepper, coat them lightly with flour, and sautée them in the hot oil till they're firm and done throughout. Be careful not to break the membrane holding the roe together. I use a wooden spoon to roll them around gently in the skillet. And be sure to keep the heat at medium or low.

Transfer the roe to a plate and pour the sherry into the skillet. Bring this to a boil on hight heat, scraping up any brown particles clinging to the bottom of the skillet. Now add the roe to the sherry, stir in the reserved onion sauce, and bring this to a boil. Reduce the heat to low, and let it simmer for 2–3 minutes. Add salt and pepper to taste.

Serve these immediately, along with a good saffron or yellow rice. Garnish them with lemon wedges and parsley or red pimiento strips.

This recipe took me quite a few times to perfect. And at the price of a shad roe, times 12. . . Well, anyway, it was worth it. I had wanted to do something a little different with shad roe, and this is it! It's so good with the sherry sauce.

Gentle handling of the sautéeing process is the key to this recipe's perfection.

Swordfish, Snapper, Cod

Swordfish Steaks with Cauliflower-and-Cheese Sauce

Serves 4–6

- 2 lbs. swordfish steaks
- 2 Tbs. melted butter
- ¼ cup sherry
- one 10-oz. pouch frozen cauliflower with cheese sauce
- ¼ cup onions, minced
- ¼ cup stuffed green olives, sliced

Place the steaks in a buttered shallow pan or baking dish and drizzle the melted butter over them. Pour sherry over them and bake at 400 degrees for at least 10 minutes. Most steaks are usually about an inch thick. If yours are thicker, adjust the time to the 10-minutes theory.

Cook the cauliflower pouch according to the directions and pour the contents into a mixing bowl with the sauce. Add the onions and sliced olives and stir them gently. Don't break up the cauliflower. Pour this over the steaks and return them to the oven for 5–7 minutes.

It's best that you bake this in a baking dish that can be placed on the table right from the oven. It's a very attractive dish, especially if you garnish it with lemon wedges and parsley.

You can also substitute halibut steaks or even thick fillets of cod, grouper, etc.

Glazed Swordfish Steaks

Serves 4–6
- 2 Tbs. Worcestershire sauce
- 2 Tbs. melted butter or margarine
- ¼ cup dark brown sugar, firmly packed
- 2 Tbs. sherry
- 2 lbs. swordfish steaks

Blend the Worcestershire sauce, butter, brown sugar, and sherry, till all the sugar is dissolved and brush the steaks on both sides with this mixture.

Brush a broiler rack with oil, lay the steaks on the rack over the broiler pan and broil them according to thickness till they flake and have lost their translucent appearance.

Place the steaks on a serving dish, then brush them with the remaining sauce, and garnish them with lemon wedges and parsley.

The sauce that you brush on tends to dry a little and gives the fish time to absorb the flavors. And there is no need to refrigerate the steaks after brushing them, provided you're going to cook them within 30–45 minutes. This works very well on halibut, too.

I've tried grilling these on a barbecue, but it doesn't work well, it burns too quickly.

Red Snapper with Livornese Sauce
(That's Italian)

Serves 2-3

 3–4 Tbs. olive oil
 1–2 Tbs. capers
  1 small can seedless black olives, pitted
  1 16 oz. can of whole tomatoes packed in
     sauce
 1–1½ lbs. red snapper fillet

Heat the olive oil in a small pan, add the capers and well drained olives and heat slowly. Now add the tomatoes, gently cutting them up with a wooden spoon, then cover this and simmer for 15 minutes.

Push the sauce aside in the pan, and lay in the snapper fillet. Lay the largest bits of sauce on top of the fillet. Cover this and cook it till the fish flakes.

This recipe was given to me by Helen Delvecchio, a friend and neighbor of mine in Royal Woods. I happened to have brought home snapper fillets the afternoon that she gave me the recipe. Since then I've tried it with grouper and flounder. Any good white fish does well with this recipe.

Not too long ago I brought home hog snapper, planning to bread it and pan-fry it. When I got home I found I didn't have a breader. I looked in my brisker and found a box of Nabisco's Nutty Wheat Thins, so I crushed a few of them in my blender. I dipped the fillets in a egg-and-milk mixture and into the crumbs and then I pan-fried them in my trusty old chicken-fryer skillet. They were delicious! Since then I've tried other things with these crushed-up crackers.

LIKE THIS: Dip the fillets in a little melted butter or margarine and then into the Wheat Thin crumbs, and broil without turning till the fish flakes nicely and turns white.

Broiled Cod with Cashew Butter

Serves 4-6

- 2 lbs. cod fillets
- Small amount of flour
- ¾ cup salted cashews
- 8 Tbs. butter or margarine, room temperature
- 1 Tbs. lemon or lime juice

Rinse and pat-dry the fillets, cut into serving-size and dust them lightly with flour. Lay them out in a single layer on a plate and refrigerate. Save the flour.

Grind the cashews in a grinder, food processor, or blender, mix them into the soft butter or margarine and the lemon or lime juice.

Remove the fish from the refrigerator and dust them again very lightly, and lay them into an oiled or buttered baking pan. The broiler pan from the oven, without the rack, will do nicely. Using a spatula, spread the cashew-butter mixture over each fillet (be generous); broil them 3–4 inches from the heat for 10 minutes per inch.

The taste of this fish-and-nut combination is excellent. Even the most hard-to-please will enjoy.

I've tried many kinds of lean white fish with this and all have been just as good as the cod. You can also make the nut-and-butter mixture ahead of time and roll it up in a plastic film and soften in the microwave or at room temperature. Or it can be melted and drizzled over the fish.

Hawaiian-Style Seafood Kabobs

Serves 6-8

- ½ cup teriyaki sauce
- ½ cup unsweetened pineapple juice
- ¼ cup safflower or peanut oil
- 1 Tbs. brown sugar
- 1 Tbs. fresh garlic, minced
- 2 tsp. ground ginger
- 1 tsp. dry mustard
- 2 lbs. firm fish in 1-inch cubes, or shrimp, etc.
- one 15-oz. can unsweetened pineapple chunks, well drained
- 1 medium-size sweet green pepper
- 1 medium-size sweet red pepper
- 12-16 large fresh mushrooms
- 18 cherry tomatoes
- 3 cups hot, cooked rice (yellow rice is best)

Bring the first seven ingredients to a boil in a medium-size saucepan, then reduce the heat and simmer for 5 minutes. Let this mixture cool, then pour into a shallow dish and add the seafood pieces, tossing them gently to coat them. Cover this and marinate it for at least an hour in the refrigerator, stirring occasionally.

Remove the seafood from the marinade, but reserve the marinade. Alternate seafood, pineapple, green pepper, mushrooms, and tomatoes on 12–16 skewers and grill these over hot coals for 15–20 minutes, or till done, turning and basting frequently with the marinade. Serve these over the rice, with a cold, crisp salad.

This dish is superb! It's so easy, and everything can be prepared in advance.

Microwave Cucumber-Sauced Salmon Steak

Serves 4

- ½ cup cucumber, chopped, peeled, and seeded
- 4 Tbs. mayonnaise (*not* salad dressing)
- 4 Tbs. sour cream
- 1 Tbs. freeze-dried chives
- 1 tsp. minced fresh onions or small amount onion powder

Salt

- 4 salmon steaks about 1-inch thick

Lemon pepper

Dried dill weed

In a bowl, mix the cucumber, mayonnaise, sour cream, chives, onions, and salt.

Put the salmon steaks in an 8-inch microwave pie plate and sprinkle them with lemon pepper. If the steaks are large you may need a 10-inch pan. Cover this with plastic wrap and cook on high for 10–12 minutes or till the fish flakes easily and is firm and opaque. Drain any liquid.

Spoon the cucumber sauce over the salmon, then sprinkle it with dried dill weed. There is no need to recover the fish. Put the microwave on defrost or the lowest setting and cook for about 5 minutes. This is just to warm the sauce.

Microwave Teriyakied Fish

Serves 2-3

- 2 Tbs. teriyaki sauce
- 2 Tbs. pineapple juice
- 1 Tbs. lemon juice
- 1 Tbs. catsup
- 1 garlic clove, finely minced
- 1 lb. grouper fillets

Combine the teriyaki sauce, pineapple and lemon juice, catsup, and garlic in a 2-quart glass baking dish. Arrange the fillets with the thick edges to the outside of the dish. Cover this with plastic wrap and microwave on high for 6–8 minutes or till the fish flakes easily. Let it stand, covered for about 5 minutes. This is delicious served with rice.

NOTE: To remove fish odors from your microwave, combine:

1	**cup water**
1	**Tbs. lemon juice**
3–4	**whole cloves**

Combine this mixture on high for about 6 minutes, longer if needed. This does the trick!

About Shark

I've always told anyone who asks that I prefer to marinate shark steaks or fillets in a commercial bottled clear Italian dressing. Or you can make your own favorite dressing. Marinate them for 2 hours or longer, even overnight, and grill or barbeque them according to thickness.

The thing to remember most about shark is that it's usually quite dry and very similar to the white meat of chicken. And, of course, don't overcook shark any more than you would any other type of fish.

In fact, if you find yourself with a large catch of shark and don't quite know what to do with it— look to your favorite chicken-breast recipes and substitute the shark meat. You won't be disappointed.

Shark is not only good grilled or broiled, but also deep-fried, stir-fried, kabobed, poached, in casseroles, curries, salads, and sauces, or "*en papillote*" (baked in oiled paper).

Shark can be used in any of the white fish recipes.

Shark is also very economical, even as popular as it has become.

Shrimp

Shrimp

American's favorite seafood, shrimp, has a distinctive taste and tender, juicy meat. The shell color of fresh shrimp varies with the species: pink, brown, or white, all of which are found in the waters of the Gulf of Mexico and the South Atlantic.

Fresh shrimp are firm in texture and have a mild odor or no odor at all. With cooked, peeled, and deveined shrimp I find that the yield is as follows:

When I steam or boil, the loss is from 35 percent to 40 percent per pound, once in a while as high as 45 percent. When you order one pound of shrimp that's cooked, peeled, and deveined, don't expect to see a whole pound of weight. The count per pound is *before* cooking.

For maximum quality, cook shrimp within one to two days of purchase. Raw headless shrimp in the shell will maintain their quality longer than cooked shrimp, and are best frozen as soon as you take them home. If fresh shrimp are frozen in a block of ice, or glazed, they will maintain their quality for up to six months. To keep them about a month (and no longer) seal them in plastic wrap or a zip lock bag, and then wrap that in freezer paper.

Rock Shrimp

Rock shrimp is a member of the shrimp family but could easily be mistaken for a miniature lobster tail. These extremely tough, rigid shellfish were for centuries the prize catch of fishermen, but today are little known to the public.

The hard shell and texture of the meat is like that of lobster, but the flavor is between lobster and shrimp.

Because rock shrimp are far more perishable than lobster or other shrimp varieties, they're usually sold in the raw, frozen state, either whole or with split tails. Unlike most Florida seafood, which is better fresh, rock shrimp are just as good and quite often better frozen. Whether you buy rock-shrimp tails fresh or frozen, you can determine their quality by their color and their odor: Good rock shrimp will have some transparent or clear white flesh with no discoloration, and the odor will be mild, with no objectionable "off odor".

Rock shrimp are sold according to size, about 21–25 per pound. Properly cleaned and cooked, one pound of peeled and deveined rock shrimp should serve six people.

How to Boil Shrimp

Bring to a boil enough water to cover the shrimp. Add any spice that you are using at the beginning. Add the shrimp when the water boils and allow the water to return to a rolling boil. Remove small shrimp at this point. Allow 2-3 more minutes for larger shrimp, and about 5 minutes (no more) for jumbos. I don't recommend adding salt to the water, because it tends to toughen the shrimp. After boiling shrimp, immediately plunge them into a bowl of ice water and let them cool completely before taking them out. This process makes them crisp and crunchy.

For a great taste, boil shrimp in beer. Use the same procedure as the water. This also eliminates any shrimp odor during cooking. And remember, all the alcohol is eliminated by the heat. Adding a few bay leaves and a lemon, squeezed and cut up, is good too.

All the above pertains to whether you peel and devein the shrimp before cooking or cook them with the shells intact.

If you don't like the smell of cooked shrimp lingering in the kitchen, put a pot of water with half a lemon and several cloves on the burner. Bring it to a boil and then allow it to simmer for a while. This procedure applies to a microwave too.

The best way to reduce odor while cooking is to add a tablespoon or two of cider vinegar to the water before adding the shrimp. This won't interfere with the taste of the shrimp. A customer once came into a seafood market where I used to work and asked for cooked shrimp. She said her husband didn't let her cook shrimp in the house because of the smell. I was out of cooked shrimp, so I convinced her to take fresh, along with the cider vinegar and the above instructions for cooking. I promised her that her husband would never know she had cooked them at home. Infact, I said, if he could tell she had cooked them at home, I would give her double her money back. Two days later she came in and said "Rose, I want another pound of those shrimp, if you'll give me the vinegar to go along with them!"

Deep-Fried Shrimp

Serves 6-8
- 1 **cup all-purpose flour**
- ½ **tsp. salt**
- ½ **tsp. sugar**
- 2 **Tbs. oil**
- 1 **egg, slightly beaten**
- 1 **cup ice water**
- 2 **lbs. shrimp, peeled and deveined, tails left on**

Combine the flour, salt, and sugar, then add the oil, egg, and ice water, and mix these well with a spoon or a whisk. Place this in the refrigerator until you're ready to use it.

Preheat oil to 350 degrees in a deep pan. Pat the shrimp dry with paper towels and holding them by the tail, dip them into the batter mix, letting excess drip off. Carefully drop the shrimp into the hot oil and fry just a few at a time, without crowding them.

The shrimp are done when they're light golden brown and when the center is opaque, not transparent. Keep the fried shrimp warm in a 250 degree oven as ya continue frying the rest. And remember to drain them on paper towels before you bake them.

Alternate-Method Fried Shrimp

Serves 3

    1   lb. shrimp peeled and deveined
1–2   cups milk, or enough to cover the shrimp
    1   cup all-purpose flour
    Salt and pepper
    4   Tbs. butter or lemon
    1   Tbs. lemon juice
    1   Tbs fresh parsley, minced

After preparing the shrimp, cover them with milk in a glass bowl and let this stand at room temperature for at least an hour.

Mix the flour, salt and pepper in a shallow dish or pie plate. Drain excess milk from the shrimp as you remove them from the dish and toll them in the flour mixture till they're well coated, shaking off any excess. Fry the shrimp without crowding, in a hot (about 350 degrees) skillet or deep fryer till they're light golden brown. Drain them on paper towels and keep them warm.

Melt the butter over medium heat in a small, heavy saucepan, and continue to cook it till it turns light golden brown, then remove it from the heat and immediately add the lemon juice and parsley. This is going to foam up quite a bit, which is normal. When the foam subsides, replace the pan on the heat and cook this for a minute or two, no longer.

Arrange the shrimp on a platter and pour the butter sauce over them. Be sure to scrape all the little brown bits onto the shrimp.

I prefer butter for this browned butter sauce, but you can use margarine. And instead of lemon juice and parsley, you can sprinkle the butter with Italian-seasoned bread crumbs. I also add fresh minced garlic at the same time as the lemon juice.

Serve these shrimp with crusty French or Italian bread to absorb all the good juices.

Coconut-Fried Shrimp

Serves 6-8

> 2 cups all-purpose flour
> 1½ cups milk
> 1½ tsp. baking powder
> 1 tsp. curry powder
> Salt
> 2 cups shredded coconut
> 2 lbs. large shrimp, peeled and deveined, with
>   tails left on

Put half a cup of the flour and the 2 cups of coconut in separate shallow dishes. In a large mixing bowl, combine the remaining flour, with the milk, baking powder, curry powder, and salt.

Dredge the shrimp in the flour, dip in the batter, then roll in the coconut, and fry in hot oil until the coconut is golden brown. Drain the shrimp on paper towels before transferring them to a warm platter. Serve them with a sweet-and-sour sauce or the one below:

- ½ cup mayonnaise
- ½ cup chili sauce
- 2 Tbs. sweet relish
- 1 tsp. mustard
- 1 tsp. dried chives
- ½ hard-boiled egg, chopped
- Salt and pepper

Mix these well and serve chilled.

Shrimp Fritters

Makes a large mixing bowl full
- 1½ lbs. large shrimp, peeled and deveined
- 1 cup all-purpose flour
- Salt
- ½ tsp. white pepper
- 1 egg
- ¾ cup half-and-half
- 2 Tbs. butter or margarine
- 1 small onion, minced
- 1 small red or green pepper, minced
- 1 small celery stalk, minced

Chop the clean shrimp finely, with a knife or in the blender or processor. Don't purée them.

Mix the flour, salt and pepper in a mixing bowl.

In another bowl, whip the egg with the half-and-half. Heat

the butter or margarine in a small skillet then add the minced vegetables and sauté them till the onions are transparent. Don't brown the vegetables.

Mix well together the shrimp, egg mixture, flour, and vegetables, and drop this by the tablespoonful into 350 degree oil. Drain the fritters on paper towels and keep them in a warm oven as you continue frying the rest.

These are great as a buffet. Serve them with a cocktail sauce, a mustard dipping sauce, or a sweet-and-sour sauce.

Simple Shrimp Fritters

Makes about 36 fritters

   1 **medium-size onion**
   1 **medium-size potato**
1½ **lbs. shrimp, peeled and deveined**
   1 **egg**
  Salt and pepper
  Garlic (optional)

Chop or mince the onions, potato, and shrimp in a blender or by hand. Stir in the egg, salt, pepper, and garlic if you choose to add it, and mix these well. The batter will be quite thick.

Drop this batter by the teaspoonful into hot oil and fry these till they're golden brown.

These are excellent served with cocktail, sweet-and-sour, or tarter sauce.

Stuffed Shrimp

Serves 4-6
- 1 lb. shrimp, large, jumbo, or colossal
- 1 pkg. Wakefield-brand crabmeat stuffing, thawed
- 2 Tbs. melted butter
- 1 tsp. lemon juice
- 1 pkg. Knorr Swiss Hollandaise sauce

Peel and devein the shrimp, leaving the tails on. Split them along the vein without cutting all the way through. Place the shrimp cut side down on a buttered shallow pan or cookie sheet, put a small amount of the crabmeat stuffing on top of each, and fold the tails over the stuffing.

Mix the 2 tablespoons of melted butter with the lemon juice, and drizzle this over the shrimp. Bake the large or jumbo shrimp for 8–10 minutes at 425 degrees, then broil them for 2–3 minutes; the colossal for 10–12 minutes, then broil for 2–3 minutes.

While the shrimp are baking/broiling, prepare the package of Hollandaise sauce according to the directions. Put a teaspoon of this on each cooked shrimp, and use the rest as a dip, or serve them plain with a squeeze of lemon.

You can also lay the shrimp on their backs, cut side up, and stuff them with the crabmeat stuffing. With this method, snip the underside in about three places to keep them from curling up in the oven.

This recipe is so simple and so good! Preparation time is very short: about 10 minutes for preparing the shrimp, and 12–15 in the oven. And you can make the Hollandaise sauce and set the table while the shrimp bake. Pop some potatoes in the microwave, add a frozen vegetable, and dinner is on the table in 30 minutes.

Shrimp and Spanish Rice

Serves 4

   3 Tbs. butter or margarine
   ½ cup sliced green onions, white and green part
   2 garlic cloves
   1 lb. fresh or frozen shrimp, peeled and deveined
 one 16-oz. can stewed tomatoes
   1 tsp. oregano leaves
   ½ cup water
 one 4½-oz. pkg. Spanish rice mix
 one 10-oz. pkg. frozen artichoke hearts
   ½ cup stuffed olives, sliced

Sauté the onions and garlic in the butter till they're wilted. Add the shrimp and sauté them till they're pink. Add the stewed tomatoes and the oregano, breaking up the tomatoes with the back of a spoon or fork, and let this simmer with a lid on for 15–20 minutes.

Add the water, rice mix, artichoke hearts, and olives, stir, and cook this for about 10 minutes, or till the rice is tender.

This is one of my favorite recipes. It's one of my old standbys.

Shrimp with Sweet Peppers And Sauce

Serves 3-4

2–3 Tbs. olive oil
1 large sweet red pepper, cut into strips
1 large sweet green pepper, cut into strips
1 medium-size banana pepper, cut into rings (optional)
2–3 garlic cloves, crushed and minced
1 lb. large or jumbo shrimp, peeled and deveined
1 cup spaghetti sauce
¼ cup fresh parsley, minced

In a large skillet, sauté the peppers and garlic till they're tender-crisp. Remove them from the pan, add the shrimp, and stir-fry them till they're about half-done.

Add the spaghetti sauce to the shrimp and let this simmer for about 5 minutes, or till the shrimp are cooked through. Return the peppers to the skillet and heat them through. Garnish this with the minced parsley, on a serving platter, and serve it with linguine, spaghetti, or fettucine.

This is a very quick dish to prepare. I clean the shrimp and prepare the peppers ahead of time and refrigerate them till I am ready to cook. The banana pepper is optional, because it's a little hot. But it's just hot enough to give this dish that little bite.

Shrimp in Creamy Tomato Sauce

Makes about 3½ cups

  1 lb. small or medium shrimp, peeled and
      deveined
2–3 shallots, minced
  1 lb. fresh tomatoes, peeled, seeded, and diced
  1 Tbs. tomato paste
  1 tsp. sugar
 ½ cup heavy whipping cream
    Salt and white pepper
  4 Tbs. unsalted butter, well-chilled

Peel and devein the shrimp. Boil enough water to cover the shrimp, drop them in, and bring them to a boil. Drain them and plunge them into ice water until they're cold through, then drain them well and set them aside.

Wash and drain the shrimp shells, combine them with the shallots, and let them simmer in a glass or enamel saucepan for about 15 minutes. Strain the liquid and discard the shells.

Return this liquid to the saucepan, add the tomatoes, tomato paste and sugar and let these simmer, stirring occasionally, until this mixture is reduced to about 1-1/4 cups.

Add the cream and the salt and papper and let this simmer for 5–7 minutes, then purée it in a blender.

Return this sauce to the same saucepan and reheat it. Cut the butter into 4 pieces and add it one piece at a time, whisking constantly till it's well blended into the sauce.

Mince the shrimp, making them smaller than dice but not mushy, and warm them enough to take the chill off. Now stir them gently into the sauce.

This is a very rich sauce, which means it goes a long way. It's great with rice or pasta, but my favorite is over homemade crêpes. It's every bit worth the extra effort.

Shrimp in Madeira Sauce

Serves 3-4

   8 Tbs. butter
   1 lb. fresh shrimp, peeled and deveined, with
        tails off
   ½ cup Madeira wine
   Salt and pepper
   ¼ cup heavy whipping cream
   ¼ cup fresh parsley, finely chopped

Melt the butter in a large, heavy skillet, add the shrimp, turning them over in the butter to coat them well, and stir-fry them till they're pink and done. Transfer them to a warm platter.

Stir the Madeira wine into the skillet, scraping the bits in the pan into the wine, and cook this mixture till the wine nearly evaporates.

Season it with salt and pepper, stir in the cream and parsley and bring it just to a boil, then reduce the heat and let it simmer for one minute.

Serve this sauce hot over the shrimp. It's great with yellow rice.

This is another of my favorite dishes. Notice that I haven't written my usual "or margarine" here. I definitely prefer the butter in this sauce. I figure since I'm using heavy whipping cream, why not butter? It works ok with margarine, but the taste with butter sure does make a difference.

Shrimp-and-Spinach Canneloni

Serves 4-6

- ¼ cup onion, minced
- 2 Tbs. butter or margarine
- one 10-oz. pkg. frozen chopped spinach, thawed and drained
- 1½ lbs. shrimp, peeled, deveined, cooked, and chopped
- ¼ cup Parmesan cheese, freshly grated
- ¼ cup Romano cheese, freshly grated
- 2 eggs, lightly beaten
- Salt and pepper
- 8 cannelloni shells, cooked according to package directions

Sauté the onion in the butter, then in a mixing bowl combine the onion with the spinach, shrimp, cheeses, and eggs. Add salt and pepper—use caution with the salt because the cheeses contain salt.

Stuff the pre-cooked shells and place them in a buttered baking dish, without crowding them. Preheat the oven to 350 degrees.

Shrimp Sauce:

- ½ lb. fresh raw uncooked shrimp, peeled and deveined
- 1 garlic clove, minced
- 4 Tbs. butter or margarine
- 4 Tbs. flour
- 2 cups half-and-half
- ¼ cup Romano cheese, freshly grated
- ¼ cup Parmesan cheese, freshly grated
- White pepper

Mince the raw shrimp in a blender and set it aside. Sauté the garlic in the butter or margarine, then add the shrimp, stirring till they're just barely cooked. Stir in the flour, then remove the pan from the heat, and gradually stir in the half-and-half. Now bring this back to a boil while stirring. Remove this from the heat as soon as it comes to a boil, and stir in the cheeses until they're melted.

Spoon this sauce over the cannelloni and bake it for about 20 minutes in the preheated oven. Then broil it till a very light golden bubble appears on the sauce.

Creamy Shrimp Crêpes

Serves 12-14 crêpes
Crêpe Batter:

   2 **eggs**
1¼ **cups milk**
   1 **cup all-purpose flour**
 ¼ **tsp. salt**
 ¼ **tsp. sugar**
   2 **Tbs. melted butter or margarine**

Blend all of the above and refrigerate it for at least an hour.

Filling:

 ½ **cup butter or margarine**
 ½ **cup all-purpose flour**
 ¼ **cup minced or dehydrated parsley**
 ¼ **cup onions, minced**
 ¼ **cup sweet red pepper, minced**
   1 **tsp. whole dried thyme, or 2 tsp.**
       fresh minced

(continued next page)

>   **2 cups milk**
>   **1 lb. fresh or frozen shrimp, peeled,**
>   **deveined, and chopped coarsely**
>   **Salt and pepper**

In a large saucepan, melt the butter or margarine, gradually stir in the flour, and cook this for about 3 minutes while stirring.

Stir in the parsley, onions, pepper, thyme, the gradually add the milk, stirring constantly. The mixture should be quite thick. Add the shrimp and continue to stir it for about 3 more minutes. Add the salt and pepper to taste.

Remove the crêpe batter from the refrigerator and stir it gently, without beating. If the batter is too thick, **stir** in a little milk.

Heat a skillet with a little oil or butter and pour about 2 tablespoons of the batter in the center, tilting the skillet to spread the mixture very thin. Cook these crêpes till the top side looks dry.

Fill each crêpe with the shrimp filling and bake them at 350 degrees for about 15 minutes. Top them with the following sauce:

Makes about 2½ cups

>   **1 can cream of shrimp soup**
>   **¼ cup cooked shrimp, finely chopped**
>   **½ cup heavy whipping cream**
>   **2 Tbs. dry sherry**
>   **1 Tbs. chopped green onion tops or freeze-**
>   **dried chives**

Blend all of these ingredients in a saucepan and heat while stirring, till it's heated through, but don't boil, or blend them in a dish and cook in a microwave on high till they're hot.

Pasta with Shrimp-and-Cheese Sauce

Serves 2-4

    1 lb. pasta (springs, shells, etc.)
    3 Tbs. olive oil
    ½ lb. small shrimp, peeled and deveined
    1 lb. ricotta cheese
    2 Tbs. unsalted butter
    Salt and pepper
    ¼ tsp. crushed red pepper
    Freshly grated Parmesan or Romano cheese

Cook the pasta according to package directions. While the pasta is cooking, make the sauce: Heat the olive oil in a large skillet, add the shrimp and sauté them till they're done, tossing them around so they cook evenly. Don't overcook these. Mix in the ricotta cheese and the unsalted butter and stir till the butter is melted then add the salt, pepper, and the hot peppers while stirring. Serve over the pasta and top with grated cheese.

This is one of those hurry-up recipes. So quick and easy, and so good!

NOTE: After peeling the shrimp, pat them dry with paper towels to keep them from spattering when you add them to the hot oil.

Shrimp Pasta Primavera

Serves 4-6

8 Tbs. butter

1 medium-size onion, minced

1 large garlic clove, minced

1 lb. asparagus

½ lb. fresh mushrooms, sliced

1 medium-sized zucchini

1 carrot

1 cup heavy cream

½ cup chicken broth

1 Tbs. dried basil

½ cup sweet red pepper

½ cup sweet green pepper

1 lb. fresh large shrimp, peeled and deveined

1 lb. fettucine, cooked and drained

1 cup grated Parmesan or Locatelli cheese

½ cup pine nuts

In a large (4-quart) Dutch oven, heat the butter, onion, and garlic, and sauté till the onion is soft and transparent.

Diagonally slice the asparagus, mushrooms, zucchini, and carrot, and stir-fry these for about 2 minutes.

Increase the heat to high, add the cream, broth, and basil and boil these till the liquid is slightly reduced. Stir in the peppers and cook for 1 minute longer.

Add the shrimp and cook till they're pink, white, and curled, then add the pasta and cheese and heat till it's hot but don't overcook it.

Serve this topped with pine nuts and more grated cheese.

Curried Shrimp á la Orange

Serves 4-6

- 1 lb. medium shrimp, peeled, and deveined
- 1 tsp. sugar
- 1 Tbs. lemon juice
- ¾ cup unsweetened orange juice
- 2 tsp. cornstarch
- 1 small can mandarin oranges, well drained
- ½ tsp. curry powder, or to taste
- 1 Tbs. freeze-dried chives, or fresh or minced parsley

For this recipe use a non-stick-coated skillet, or a regular skillet coated with vegetable spray. Heat the skillet and stir-fry the shrimp till they just turn opaque and have a nice pink color, then remove them from the skillet.

Sprinkle the sugar over the bottom of the skillet, add the lemon juice, and cook this mixture while stirring till it turns light golden brown. Be careful with this because it will burn very quickly.

Mix the orange juice and cornstarch and pour them into the skillet while stirring. Add the mandarin oranges, cooked shrimp, and curry powder and stir these very gently.

Serve this with chives or parsley.

I put this recipe together when I went on one of my frequent diets. There isn't any added fat, and the very small amount of sugar used with the lemon juice is hardly worth mentioning. This dish is so good, and good for you. It's just as delicious without the curry, too.

Barbequed Shrimp

Serves 4-6

  24 large or jumbo shrimp, peeled and deveined
          with tails left on
  12 bacon strips, cut in half
   1 bottle commercial barbeque sauce

Fry the bacon strips till they're limp (leave on some of the fat) and then drain them on paper towels. Or cook them in the microwave.

Wrap the half-strips of bacon around each shrimp (excluding the tails) and fasten them with toothpicks. Spread the barbeque sauce in the bottom of a shallow dish and lay the shrimp in the sauce, brushing the tops with more sauce. Refrigerate these for several hours or overnight—even one hour will do.

Grill or broil the shrimp for 3–4 minutes on each side, brushing them with the barbeque sauce.

The shrimp can also be threaded onto a skewer. This makes turning them a lot faster. (And eliminates the chance of losing any to the coals.) And leave the tails on; you'll need a "handle" to hold them with. Talk about finger-lickin' good!

Grilled Teriyakied Shrimp

Makes 4 appetizers or 2 main courses

  1 cup teriyaki sauce
  1 cup pineapple juice
  4 Tbs. butter or margarine, melted
  1 lb. jumbo shrimp

Mix the teriyaki sauce, pineapple juice, and butter in a glass bowl.

Peel and devein the shrimp, leaving the tails intact. Score the **underside** of each shrimp crosswise, to keep them from curling when cooking. Stir the sauce mixture before laying the shrimp in the bowl and marinate this for at least an hour.

Grill the shrimp over hot coals, turning them till they're pink and done. The time depends on the heat of your coals and the size of your shrimp.

Pickled Shrimp

Serves 12–18 for hors d'oeuvres, or 8–12 for cocktails

   2 cups white distilled vinegar
  ½ cup sugar
   1 Tbs. salt, or to taste
   2 tsp. fresh, cracked pepper
   4 Tbs. pickling spice

Mix all the ingredients in a medium-size saucepan. Bring this to a boil, then reduce the heat to a simmer for about 15 minutes. Now let it cool.

2–3 lbs. shrimp, peeled, deveined, and cooked, tails left on
   1 large lemon, thinly sliced
   2 medium-size red onions, thinly sliced
   2 medium-size sweet red peppers, sliced into rings
   2 medium-size sweet green peppers, sliced into rings

Layer the shrimp, onions, lemon slices, and pepper rings

in a non-metallic bowl and pour in the cooked-and-cooled mixture. Refrigerate this for about 8 hours or overnight. If all of the ingredients are not immersed in the liquid, you'll need to stir them occasionally.

To serve these as hors d'oeuvres, drain off the liquid and arrange the shrimp and vegetables on a platter.

To serve them as individual shrimp cocktails, arrange the shrimp and vegetables on a lettuce-lined salad plate or bowl.

The pickled shrimp are best within 3 days of refrigerating them, though they will keep for 7 days. If kept longer, the shrimp get tough and the vegetables get wimpy.

Once you try these, you'll have to have them again and again.

Crab

Garlic-Butter-Sautéed Soft-Shell Blue Crabs

Serves 5

  10 **prepared soft-shell blue crabs, fresh or frozen**
      Salt and pepper
      A small amount all-purpose flour
    8 **Tbs. butter or margarine**
4–6 **garlic cloves, crushed**
    2 **tsp. lemon juice**
    2 **Tbs. fresh parsley, chopped**
      A few dashes Worcestershire sauce

Rinse and pat-dry the crabs, sprinkle with salt and pepper, and dust them lightly with flour. Heat the butter or margarine in a skillet, then add the crushed garlic and the crabs and cook them gently till both sides of the crabs are reddish. Put the crabs on a warm platter.

Add the lemon juice, parsley, and Worcestershire sauce to the skillet and heat for a minute or two. Pour this over the crabs.

Soft-Shell Crabs in Marinara Sauce with Cheese

Follow the above recipe for sautéeing the crabs. Heat the Marinara Sauce (which see) slightly and pour it over the crabs. Sprinkle them with a fresh grated combination of Parmesan and Romano cheeses and broil this till the cheese melts and the sauce bubbles. Serve this with a crisp garlic toast or bread.

Imitation-Crab Stir-Fry

Serves 6 (generous)

    2 Tbs. peanut oil
    2 large garlic cloves, cut in half
  ½ lb. fresh mushrooms, thinly sliced
    6 small zucchini, thinly sliced
    1 lb. imitation crab, cut into medium-size chunks
one 8-oz. can sliced water chestnuts, well-drained
    3 Tbs. oyster sauce
  ½ cup green onion, thinly sliced

Heat the oil in a wok or heavy skillet, add the garlic and cook it on medium till it begins to brown, then remove it.

Turn the heat to high and cook the mushrooms and zucchini till they're tender-crisp, stirring constantly.

Add the crabmeat and water chestnuts and cook till heated through. Now add the oyster sauce and heat through, stirring gently.

Serve this over rice or pilaf.

Crab-Stuffed Mushrooms (1)

Makes 18

  ½ cup chopped onion
    2 Tbs. celery, minced
  ¼ cup chopped sweet red or green pepper
    1 Tbs. fresh parsley, chopped
    2 Tbs. melted butter or margarine
  ½ tsp. thyme
    5 dashes hot sauce, or to taste
Salt and pepper

(continued next page)

½ lb. crabmeat
1 cup Italian-seasoned bread crumbs
18 large fresh mushrooms
Paprika for garnish

Sauté the onion, celery, pepper, and parsley in the butter or margarine, add the thyme, hot sauce, salt, pepper, crabmeat, and bread crumbs and mix this well.

Remove the mushrooms and stems and put them aside (you can use them with the recipe that follows).

Spoon the above mixture into the mushroom caps, sprinkle them with paprika, drizzle melted butter or margarine over them, and bake them uncovered at 350 degrees for about 10–15 minutes.

You can also sprinkle these with grated Parmesan cheese just before baking, if you like the cheesy flavor.

Crab-Stuffed Mushrooms (2)

Makes 25-30
1 large pkg. large fresh mushroms
2 green onions, finely chopped
½ green pepper, finely chopped
1 lb. crabmeat
1 cup mayonnaise
1 tsp. horseradish
1 tsp. Worcestershire sauce
1 cup Italian-style bread crumbs

Chop the mushroom stems and sauté them in a little butter

or margarine. Add the onions and green pepper and cook till they're tender.

Mix the rest of the ingredients. Use a little water if needed to moisten.

Stuff the mushroom caps and bake them on a buttered cookie sheet for about 15 minutes at 375 degrees.

Crab Imperial

Serves 4-6

4 Tbs. butter or margarine	Salt and pepper
2 Tbs. green pepper, minced	1½ cups milk
2 Tbs. sweet red pepper, minced	2 Tbs. dry sherry
¼ cup all-purpose flour	2 egg yolks, room temperature
1 tsp. dry mustard	1 lb. jumbo lump blue-crabmeat (or backfin)
1 tsp. Worcestershire sauce	

Melt the butter in a medium-size saucepan and sauté the peppers till they're tender-crisp. Stir in the flour, mustard, Worcestershire sauce, salt, and pepper and blend these well. Slowly add the milk and the sherry while stirring till the sauce thickens and comes to a boil, then remove the saucepan from the heat. Meanwhile preheat the broiler.

Beat the egg yolks slightly in a small bowl, stir in about a quarter of the above hot sauce, then slowly pour this egg mixture back into the saucepan, whisking quickly to prevent any lumps. Now fold in the crabmeat.

Put this mixture in buttered crab shells or individual baking dishes, and broil just till they're bubbly and hot.

Crabcakes

Serves 4-6

- 2 lbs. claw crab meat
- 2 whole eggs, slightly beaten
- 1 medium-size onion, minced
- 1 medium-size sweet red pepper, minced
- 2 Tbs. Old Bay seasoning
- 2 Tbs. dry mustard
- 2 Tbs. Worcestershire sauce or Picapeppa sauce
- 1½–2 cans of Italian-seasoned bread crumbs
- 2–3 cups mayonnaise

Mix all of these ingredients, adjusting the amount of bread crumbs and mayonnaise to make a firm consistency, and form this batter into cakes. You can wet your hands with water or oil to aid you in making them.

Grill or pan-fry the cakes in butter or margarine until they're golden brown on both sides. (they don't lend themselves well to deep-frying.)

These cakes are excellent served as a main course with any sauce you like on the side or as sandwiches with toasted buns, wafer cakes, or saltines.

I suggest you refrigerate the crabmeat mixture for about two hours before cooking, but no longer than four hours—the flavors will blend too well and the crab flavor will be overwhelmed.

About Stone-Crab Claws

If you're not from Florida, or haven't vacationed there, you may not have heared about stone crabs. Cosidered a delicacy in Florida, they're harvested commercially only in Florida waters from October 15 to May 15. You might find them frozen, but don't depend on it; the seasonal demand for stone crab is usually greater than the supply. The sweet white meat is even more delicate in flavor than lobster.

Here are a few ways to enjoy stone crab claws (if you can get them):

Hot Stone-Crab Claws with Warm Mustard Sauce

Allow 1¼ lbs. of crab claws per person
- ½ cup sour cream
- 1½ Tbs. Dijon mustard
- 2 tsp. melted butter or margarine
- ½ tsp. parsley flakes
- Pinch of salt

Mix all these ingredients and warm them on low heat or in the microwave, stirring occasionally, but don't let it boil.

Drop them into a pot of boiling water long enough just to warm them. (Stone crab claws are already cooked when you buy them.) Then carefully crack them with a small hammer or the back of a butcher knife. Hit them as if you were hitting a piece of glass. Serve them with the mustard sauce. They're also delicious served with drawn butter.

Cold Stone-Crab Claws with
Cold Mustard Sauce

½ cup sour cream
½ cup mayonnaise (*not* salad dressing)
¼ cup Dijon mustard
1 Tbs. dry mustard
Dash Worcestershire sauce
1 tsp. turmeric powder

Mix all these ingredients and refrigerate for a little while to let the flavors blend. (Turmeric is just for color, not taste.)
Crack and serve the claws cold with the sauce.

Stone Crabs á la Marinara

Serves 2-4

2 cups basic marinara sauce (which see)
Dash or two Tabasco sauce
2½ lbs. stone-crab claws, cracked and with meat
picked out of claws

Heat the basic marinara sauce with the Tabasco sauce and the stone-crab meat, gently and slowly, without overcooking.
This is delicious served with a good crusty French or Italian bread, over linguine or spaghetti.

Crab Louis with Dressing

Makes 4–6 salad plates

- ½ cup mayonnaise, commercial or homemade
- 2 Tbs. chili sauce
- 2 Tbs. green onion, chopped
- 1 hard-boiled egg, chopped
- 1 Tbs. stuffed green olives, minced

Dash lemon juice

Salt and pepper

- 1 lb. crabmeat, preferably jumbo lump and fresh

Mix all the above except the crabmeat with a wire whip, chill and pour over the crabmeat on a bed of lettuce or fresh spinach leaves.

I have used stone-crab claws in place of the jumbo lump, and it's scrumptious! It's just as good with Alaskan King crabmeat, and imitation crabmeat almost indistinguishable from king crab. (Almost.)

Alaska King-Crab Legs Marinara

Makes enough sauce for 1–1½ lbs. spaghetti

- 2 lbs. Alaskan king-crab legs, thawed and removed from shells
- 2 cups basic marinara sauce (which see)

Hold the frozen crab legs under running water till they're completely thawed, heat the sauce and add the crabmeat but don't cook it.

Thawing them this way helps rid them of excess salt; Alaskan king-crab legs are cooked on the boat when they are caught, right in the seawater they came out of. So they tend to be on the salty side.

Deviled Crabs

Serves 8-10

- 1 lb. crabmeat (with the shells)
- ¼ cup sweet green pepper, minced
- ¼ cup sweet red pepper, minced
- 1 Tbs. onion, chopped
- 1 Tbs. lemon juice
- 1½ cups packaged breadcrumbs (or your own)
- 1 cup cream or half-and-half
- 3 hard-boiled eggs, chopped
- 1 Tbs. dry mustard
- 1 Tbs. Worcestershire sauce
- ½ cup mayonnaise, (*not* salad dressing)
- 8 Tbs. butter or margarine melted and cooled
- Salt and pepper
- 1 or 2 dashes Tabasco (optional)

Make sure the crabmeat is free of shell and cartilage, then mix all of these ingredients. If the mixture seems a little too wet, add a few more bread crumbs. Pack the mixture into buttered crab shells and press the shells into a rectangular baking dish with crumpled foil in the bottom, to keep them upright. Bake these at 400 degrees for about 10 minutes or till they're golden brown.

You can brush the individual crabs with melted butter and paprika before baking if you like. Also, if you like deep-fried stuffed crabs, after stuffing each crab shell, roll them in bread crumbs, baking mix, or pancake mix and deep-fry them till golden brown.

I always serve a large lemon wedge with these. They're also good with cocktail or tartar sauce, even a well-seasoned white sauce.

Crabby Deviled Eggs

Makes 2-4
- 1 dozen hard-boiled eggs (see below)
- ½ lb. crabmeat
- ½ cup mayonnaise (*not* salad dressing)
- 2 Tbs. cider vinegar
- 1 tbs. dry mustard
- Salt and pepper

Cut the eggs in half lengthwise, and remove and mash the yolks thoroughly. Add the remaining ingredients to the yolk-mash and mix well. Put this into the egg halves and dust them lightly with paprika.

How to Boil an Egg

Place a dozen eggs, preferably at room temperature, in a large pot, cover them with cold water, and add one table-spoon of salt or vinegar. Put a lid on the pot, bring it to a full rolling boil, remove it from the heat, leaving the lid on and let it cool, for a minimum of 20 minutes without disturbing it. Now pour off the hot water and cover the eggs with ice water. When they're cold, crack and peel them under running water. You should have a perfect hard-cooked egg, no greenish gray around the yolk.

Now I'll tell you what can happen when you boil an egg too long. Way too long. I put some eggs on to boil once in a restaurant where I worked and then got too busy somewhere else and totally forgot about the eggs. All of a sudden loud "pops" and "bangs" come from the kitchen. Everyone ran for the kitchen and, lo and behold those eggs were exploding like grenades. All over the ceiling, the stove hood, the counters—everything was covered with egg and little pieces of shell were embedded in anything they could penetrate. Then someone said "Rose, don't you know you never, never **boil** an egg, let alone 4 dozen of them?" I know now.

Lobster

About the Cooking
of Lobster Tails

2 lobster tails, 12—14 ounces each
1 large pot
Melted butter

Thaw the tails first, if frozen. Bring water to a boil in the pot (enamel, glass, or stainless steel—**not** aluminum). You can add half a lemon or lime, rind and all, but don't add any salt. A bay leaf is good, too. Drop the thawed tails into the pot, cover it with a tight-fitting lid, and cook no longer than 8 minutes from the time you've put the lid on. Remove the tails and run cool water on them just till you can handle them rather easily, but not too cold. Now preheat the broiler.

Using kitchen shears, cut the shell all the way back to the fins, spread the shell apart, and loosen the meat from the shell. Lay the meat on top of the shell or stuff it inside. If you put the meat inside the shell, make sure the shell is spread open. The tail where you have cut it should look transparent. This will finish cooking under the broiler.

Brush the tails with butter and lay them on a broiler rack and pan, or on crushed aluminum foil in the broiler pan, pressing the tails down into the foil. Now broil them for 5–8 minutes, keeping a close eye on them. Do **not** overcook them. I suggest that you hang on to the oven door—*stay right there!* I've gone across the kitchen to do something else, and stayed away too long. You don't want to brown the tails, just finish cooking them.

Serve them immediately with drawn butter or margarine— there are lots of good margarines on the market that can be clarified and are just as tasty as butter.

Lobster Newburg

Serves 4-6

  5 Tbs. butter or margarine
  3 Tbs. all-purpose flour
1½ cups cream or half-and-half
    Salt and pepper
  1 lb. cooked lobster meat, chopped
2–3 Tbs. sherry

Melt the butter in a heavy saucepan, blend in the flour, add the cream slowly, in a steady stream, whisking gently till it's smooth, and cook this till the sauce is thick, stirring constantly. Add the salt, pepper, and paprika and stir well. Add the lobster and cook this till the lobster is heated through but not cooked. Remove it from the heat and slowly stir in about 2 tablespoons of the sherry. Add more sherry to your taste if you like.

Butter individual lobster shells and serve the sauce in these with toast points or in a serving dish with toast points separately.

This is an easy and quick-to-prepare dish. It can be served very plainly or as elegantly as you wish.

Lobster Thermidor

Serves 4

- 2 live Maine lobsters, 1¼–1½ lbs. each
- 4 Tbs. butter or margarine
- ½ cup fresh mushrooms, thinly sliced
- ½ cup bread crumbs
- 2 egg yolks, slightly beaten
- Salt and pepper
- 1 tsp. dry mustard
- 1 Tbs. fresh parsley, minced
- ½ small, sweet red pepper, finely minced
- 3–4 dashes Worcestershire sauce
- 1–3 dashes hot sauce (optional)
- ¼ cup white wine
- 2 Tbs. sherry, brandy, or cognac
- 1 cup heavy whipping cream
- ½ cup Romano and Parmesan cheese, freshly grated

Cook the lobsters, and cool them so they can be handled easily. Split the lobsters in half, remove the meat from the claws and tail and any in the body section, chop the meat coarsely, and rinse and dry the shells.

Melt the butter or margarine in a large, heavy saucepan and sauté the mushrooms for about 3 minutes. Add the bread crumbs, egg yolks, salt, and pepper. Don't stir these, just toss them around in the pan. Add the mustard and gently toss again. Add the lobster meat, parsley, pepper, hot sauce and Worcestershire, and gently toss again. Add the wine and sherry and continue to heat for about a minute, then gradually add the cream, using a gentle tossing motion, without stirring or beating.

Divide the filling evenly among the four shells. Set the

lobster halves down into crushed aluminum foil on a broiler pan, to keep them upright, and sprinkle them with Romano and Parmesan cheeses. Drizzle a little melted butter on them if you like. Now broil them about 4 inches from the heat till bubbly on the edges and golden brown on top.

This is undoubtedly the finest of all lobster dishes. It will stay nice and fluffy, provided you don't stir or beat the mixture; that's what makes it so great.

Fried Lobster Tail *(That's right--fried!)*

I'll just talk you through this one. Bear with me and you'll enjoy a version of lobster that you would never think possible.

First, thaw the tails if frozen. Cut the shell so you can remove the tail in one piece. Cut the tail in half, lengthwise, and cut each half into bite-size sections. Toss the pieces in a flour, salt, and pepper mixture, shaking off any excess. Beat one egg and one tablespoon of water or milk, dip the lobster pieces into this, letting any excess drain off, and roll them in seasoned bread crumbs. Fry them in oil for about 3 minutes. Cook them in batches so they're not overcrowded. Drain them on paper towels and keep them warm.

These can be used as a main course or as hors d'oeuvres. Serve them with a good cocktail sauce, tartar sauce, sweet-and-sour sauce, honey, or a honey-mustard sauce. I find this excellent with the mustard sauce, that I usually serve with Florida stone-crab claws.

If you're serving this as a main course, count on a 12-ounce tail per person. As an appetizer, you can approximate the amount you need by each lobster tail. Just remember—do not overcook!

Lobster Tails á la Marsala

Serves 2-4

- 1–1½ lbs. lobster tails, fresh or frozen
- 2 Tbs. butter or margarine
- ½ lb. fresh mushrooms, thinly sliced
- 1 small sweet green pepper, diced
- 1 small can roasted sweet red peppers, rinsed and chopped
- ½ cup Marsala wine
- 1 can cream-of-shrimp soup

Thaw the tails if frozen. Bring water to a boil in a large pot, drop in the lobster tails, and boil for 4–6 minutes for small tails, 5–10 for large. Don't overcook them.

Cool them under cold running water and with kitchen shears, cut away the underside membrane on both sides and remove it. Pull the meat out in one piece and cut it crosswise into half-inch slices. (Save the shells.)

In a skillet, heat the butter and sauté mushrooms and green pepper till they're soft. Add the lobster slices and cook them for about a minute. Add the roasted peppers and Marsala wine and set it aflame. Now stir in the soup and continue to heat the mixture just till it bubbles.

Spoon this into the shells and garnish them with lemon and parsley.

I had eaten at a restaurant that served lobster similar to this, and asked the chef if he would part with his recipe. He said no. So I went home and put this dish together, and I swear it's better than the one that I had eaten in the restaurant. I'm glad he said no.

Fantastic Florida Lobster Tails
(Never really figured out what to call this except fantastic)

Serves 8

- 8 Florida lobster tails, about 6 ounces each
- 1 small green pepper, chopped
- 2 Tbs. pimiento, chopped
- 2 tsp. dry mustard
- 2 egg yolks
- 1 cup mayonnaise (*not* salad dressing)

Salt and pepper

Cut along the undersides of the lobster tails and remove the meat. Save the shells. Dice or cut the tail into bite-size pieces. Combine the lobster meat with the rest of the ingredients and mix this gently. Heap this mixture back into the tails, top them with another dollop of mayonnaise, or sprinkle them with paprika. Gently push the tails down into crumpled aluminum foil in a baking dish, to keep them upright and bake them at 350 degrees for about 15 minutes, or till the lobster is fully cooked and the sauce is bubbly.

This is great cold or slightly warmed, but it's best hot right out of the oven.

Microwave Lobster Tail

- one 12–14 oz. lobster tail
- 2 bamboo skewers
- 1 sheet wax paper or plastic film
- 1 microwave-proof plate
- 1 microwave

Split the lobster tail down to the fins and loosen it from the shell. Nip the edges of the thin line running along the underneath with scissors or a knife. Insert skewers all the way through the tail, and cook it on medium high for six minutes on each side. Now, this is with my microwave. All microwaves vary. You can also cook it with butter and sprinkle with paprika.

Mollusks
(oysters, clams, scallops, conch, mussels)

Oysters and Clams

Oysters on the Avocado Half-Shell

Makes 3 main courses or 6 appetizers

- 4 Tbs. butter or margarine, melted
- 1 Tbs. lemon juice
- 3 small to medium-ripe avocados, split in half, seeded but not peeled
- 1 pint fresh oysters
- White pepper
- 4 strips thin bacon, cooked crisp and crumbled
- 6 Tbs. Parmesan and Romano cheeses, freshly grated
- 3 Tbs. Italian-seasoned bread crumbs
- Minced parsley or paprika

Mix the melted butter with the lemon juice and dip the cut sides of the avocado halves in this mixture; this is so the avocados don't turn brown. Set the butter mixture aside.

Pat the oysters dry with paper towels, but don't rinse them. Put 2 or 3 oysters in each avocado half-shell, sprinkle them with white pepper, and top them with the crumbled bacon. Mix the cheeses and the bread crumbs together and spread these on top of the oysters. Drizzle the butter-lemon mixture over all.

Set the avocado halves down into crumpled foil in a shallow baking dish or pan so they sit level, and bake them at 400 degrees for 12–15 minutes, just till the edges of the oysters start to curl.

Serve these with the parsley or paprika and with a good garlic toast.

If you have an oyster-lover in the house, he's going to love you for making this. This is good with a hot sauce too.

Oysters Rockefeller

Makes 18 shells

- one 10-oz. pkg. frozen spinach, chopped
- 8 Tbs. butter or margarine
- ¼ cup celery, finely minced
- ¼ cup green onion, finely minced
- 2 Tbs. fresh parsley, chopped
- 2 Tbs. anisette liqueur
- ½ cup bread crumbs
- Salt and pepper
- 1 pint select oysters
- 18 baking shells or oyster half-shells

Cook the spinach according to the package directions, then pour it into a colander and immediately pour ice water over it. Drain it and squeeze the excess water out.

Mix all of the above ingredients with the spinach except the oysters and shells. Place an oyster in each shell and top these with the spinach mixture.

Mix the following ingredients

- ¼ cup bread crumbs
- ¼ cup grated Parmesan cheese
- 2 Tbs. butter or margarine, melted

Arrange the oyster shells on a cookie sheet covered with crumpled foil, pressing them into the foil so they stay upright. Top each oyster with the bread crumb-and-cheese mixture and bake at 450 degrees till the crumbs turn light golden brown and the edges of the oysters start to curl.

Also, if you like, cook a few strips of bacon till they're crisp, drain them well on paper towels, crumble them and sprinkle them on top of the spinach mixture or mix them into the bread crumb, cheeses, and butter mixture.

Zippy Broiled Oysters

Serves 6 (at 4 per person)

- 24 oyster half-shells
- 8 Tbs. melted butter or margarine
- 2 Tbs. Pickapeppa sauce
- 1 Tbs. lemon juice
- 4 slices fresh bread
- 2 Tbs. Parmesan cheese, freshly grated
- Paprika for garnish
- About 48 garlic-flavored Melba toast rounds

Place the shucked oyster halves on a bed of ice and refrigerate them. Blend the butter, Pickapeppa sauce, and lemon juice till they're well mixed and put this aside.

Clean and dry the blender. Cut the 4 slices of bread into cubes and blend them half at a time. Bake these crumbs in a shallow baking pan at 400 degrees for about 3 minutes, then stir them before baking them further till they're light golden brown and crispy. This should take about 6 minutes.

Place the oyster half-shells into crumpled foil on a cookie sheet so they sit evenly. Whip the butter, Pickapeppa sauce, and lemon mixture again so it's well mixed and spoon it evenly over the oysters. Bake these at 400 degrees for about 12 minutes.

While the oysters are baking, combine the toasted bread crumbs with the Parmesan cheese.

Remove the oysters from the oven, spoon the crumb-and-cheese mixture onto each oyster, sprinkle them with paprika, and bake them again for about 3 minutes, or till they're light golden brown.

Serve these with the Melba toast rounds as an appetizer.

If you have rock salt on hand, you can use it instead of the crumpled aluminum foil. Preheat the pan of rock salt in the oven, place the oysters on it, and reduce the baking time to about 10 minutes, or till the edges of the oysters start to curl.

You can also eliminate grating your own cheese and making your own bread crumbs by using pre-packaged; either plain or Italian-seasoned bread crumbs work fine. For me, it depends on how much time I have and how well prepared I am for guests. Whichever way you make this, it really whets the appetite.

Marinated Oyster-Pineapple Hors d'oeuvres

Makes 18-24
- one   16-oz. can select oysters, drained
- 1   large can pineapple chunks, packed in natural juices, not in syrup
- 10–12 bacon strips, cut in half and partially fried or microwaved

Wrap a half-strip of limp bacon around each oyster and pineapple chunk and fasten this with a toothpick. Marinate these for 15 minutes—2 hours (no longer) in the following:

- ½   cup unsweetened pineapple juice
- ½   cup Teriyaki sauce

Bake these on a broiler rack and pan at 400 degrees for about 12–15 minutes and serve them hot.

Clam Fritters

Serves 6–8

- 24 top-neck clams
- ½ cup clam juice
- 2 cups all-purpose flour
- 1 Tbs. baking powder
- 1 Tbs. minced onion
- 2 eggs, lightly beaten
- 1 cup milk
- 2 Tbs. vegetable oil
- Dash Tabasco sauce (optional)
- Salt

Shuck the clams and drain them in a colander, reserving the juice, then coarsely chop them.

Mix the flour, baking powder, and onion. Mix the eggs, milk, oil and *half* the clam juice.

Combine the flour mixture and the liquids until they're smooth, then stir in the chopped clams. The mixture should be thick enough to drop from a spoon. If it's too thick, add clam juice gradually, till you get the right consistency. If it's too thin, add a very small amount of flour. (This will vary because clams don't all hold the same amount of liquid.)

Heat a deep-fryer to 350 degrees, drop the batter by teaspoonfuls into the hot oil and fry for about 3 minutes or till they're light golden brown. Drain these on paper towels, and keep them warm in the oven while you finish cooking.

HINT: Dip your spoon into the hot oil very quickly and then into the batter and use another spoon to slide the batter into the oil. You'll find that the batter slides off the spoon very easily. I keep two iced-teaspoons just for this purpose.

If you don't like the idea of shucking clams, ask your seafood market for a pint already shucked.

The Case of The Iniquitous Rat versus The Inimitable Clam

This is a strange tale told by a Virginia country gentleman turned seafood entrepreneur. His name is Garland Edwards. Age unverifiable, and he won't tell. And no one bothers to ask anymore.

Back in the early 40's, before the time of large-scale refrigeration, Garland and his friend and partner owned and operated a seafood market in Alexandria, Virginia. His partner Jack is the only one who can verify this story. Of course, neither one was about to tell it when it actually happened. Who wants to admit he has a rat in the basement? Of course, neither actually saw what happened. Garland's testimony of the scene is based only on circumstantial evidence, but is highly reliable, nonetheless.

At the closing of each business day, Garland would remove the clams from the showcase and take them to the basement to make them a home for the night. He would hose down the floor, which had a drain pipe which emptied into the alley outside. He would then lay out burlap bags, lay the clams on them, throw a layer of ice over the clams and cornmeal on the ice. Garland said this provided the clams with the wet, cool atmosphere they need, and the cornmeal was food to fatten them up.

Well, one evening after he did his ritual with the clams and everybody had gone, quite a bizarre chain of events took place.

Enter one determined, iniquitous rat through the drain-pipe. After all, the odor of the clam juice mixed with the cornmeal has great enticing powers over such critters. The rat proceeded to feast on the cornmeal and, as you know, clams do open their shells. Especially for a delicacy such as cornmeal. While the rat was having his king's ransom of a feast, his tail happened to cross an open clamshell. The shell snapped shut with the touch of that tail, imperviously, holding on to it for eternity.

The rat feverishly tried to rid his tail of the clam, running in circles, flinging all the clams on the burlap bags in a complete circle. The center of the circle became the arena of battle for the rat and the clam.

The rat, deciding he could not win in this gladiator's circle made a direct, fast exit for the drainpipe. He fit, but the clam didn't. In his frenzy, the rat didn't think about the thing attached to his tail. The fortitude of the clam triumphed.

The scene, as Garland came upon it the next morning, is very explicit: The disreputable rat caught in the drainpipe by the noble clam.

This is what I call "caught dead to rights," "caught in the act," or in Garland's epitome—"The Clam that Killed the Rat."

Scallops

Scallops in Wine Sauce

Serves 4-6

- 1 lb. sea or bay scallops
- 1 cup dry white wine
- 4 Tbs. butter
- 2 green onions, sliced, with tops
- ½ lb. fresh mushrooms, thinly sliced
- 2 Tbs. all-purpose flour
- ¼ cup heavy whipping cream
- Ramekins or scallop shells

In a heavy saucepan, simmer the scallops in the white wine for about 3–5 minutes, or till they become opaque, then remove them and save the wine.

In the same pan, melt the butter and sauté green onions and the mushrooms without overcooking them, then remove them and set them aside.

Stir the flour into the pan, add the cream and wine, heat this through, then return the scallops, mushrooms, and onions and cook while stirring till it's heated through.

Divide this among the ramekins or scrubbed shells, sprinkle with a little Parmesan cheese, and broil them just till the cheese turns golden brown. (This won't take long, so don't leave the oven.)

This can be made ahead of time. Just add the cheese when you are ready to broil.

Scallops in Rosemary-Wine Sauce

Serves 4

- 1 lb. sea scallops
- ¼ cup flour
- 1 garlic clove, or to your taste
- *1 Tsp. Rosemary
- 8 Tbs. butter or margarine
- ½ cup dry white wine
- Lemon wedges

Sauté the garlic and rosemary in butter, remove the garlic, dust the scallops with flour, and stir-fry them in the butter making sure they don't stick, till they're light golden brown.

Put the scallops on a warm plate, add the wine to the butter, stir, and let it simmer till the liquid is reduced to about a quarter cup, then return the scallops to the skillet to warm them in the sauce. Serve these immediately with lemon wedges.

*I put the rosemary in the blender to pulverize them—I love the flavor of rosemary but I don't like the bitter taste when I bite into one of the leaves.

Scallops with Pecan and Cracker-Meal Breading

Serves 4

- ⅓ cup flour
- 1 egg
- 2 Tbs. milk
- ⅔ cup cracker meal·
- ½ cup ground pecans
- 1 lb. sea scallops
- Vegetable oil
- Salt and pepper

Mix the flour, salt, and pepper in a pie plate, the eggs and milk in a bowl, and the cracker meal and ground pecans in another pie plate.

Dust the scallops in the flour, dip them in the egg and milk, then roll them in the pecan and cracker meal.

Heat the oil in a skillet and sauté the scallops until golden brown. Serve them with lemon wedges.

I put the pecans in the blender and grind them till they're as fine as the cracker meal.

Coquilles Saint Jacques
(Pronounced Co-KEY Sawn Zshawk)

Serves 6

1½ lbs. fresh sea scallops	1 cup fresh mushrooms, chopped
1 cup dry white wine	2 Tbs. flour
1 Tbs. lemon juice	½ cup milk
2 sprigs parsley	2 egg yolks
1 bay leaf	½ cup light cream
½ tsp. salt	1 cup soft bread crumbs
2 Tbs. butter	2 Tbs. melted butter
2 Tbs. shallots, thinly sliced	

First, halve or quarter any large scallops. Then in a saucepan combine the scallops, wine, lemon juice, parsley, bay leaf, and salt, and bring this to a boil. Reduce the heat, cover it, and let it simmer for 2–4 minutes, or till the scallops are opaque, then remove them and strain the wine mixture through a fine-mesh strainer. Reserve one cup of the liquid.

Heat a skillet with 2 tablespoons of butter, add the shallots and mushrooms, and cook for about 5 minutes, or till they're tender. Stir in the flour, add salt and pepper to taste (if at all), add the reserve liquid and the milk, and cook while stirring till this is thick and bubbly, then remove it from the heat.

Whisk the egg yolks and cream together well. Gradually stir about half the hot mixture into the egg yolk mixture, return this to the remaining hot mixture in the skillet, add the scallops, and heat this while stirring just till it's bubbly. Then reduce the heat and stir over low heat for about 2 minutes longer.

If you don't have any coquilles, you can use 6-ounce custard dishes or individual casseroles. Spoon the scallop mixture into these, sprinkle with a mixture of bread crumbs and 2 table-spoons of melted butter, and bake at 400 degrees for about 10 minutes, or till they're browned.

I like to serve these with stuffed artichokes. The two just seem to go together. Add fresh-baked rolls or croissants and a nice light salad.

And for dessert I use fresh fruit, sliced kiwi, pineapple chunks, seedless green grapes, strawberries, and fresh mint-leaves, all marinated in Cointreau Liqueur. Place the fruit in serving dishes and just before serving add a scoop of orange sherbet, with a whole strawberry, stem and leaves intact, on top of the sherbet. This is very simple and very impressive with all the colors. Serve a plain but not-too-sweet biscuit with the fruit.

Marinated And Broiled Scallops

Serves 4
- 2 lbs. large sea scallops
- ½ cup dry vermouth
- ½ cup olive oil
- ½ tsp. garlic powder, or less if desired
- 3 Tbs. dehydrated or fresh parsley
- Salt and pepper

Mix all these ingredients well in a glass or ceramic bowl and refrigerate this for several hours—anywhere from 1 to 6 hours.

Broil the marinated scallops 2–4 inches from the heat for 2–3 minutes on one side, then 5–6 on the other. The scallops are done when they are opaque all the way through.

A dry white wine may be used if you don't have vermouth.

Conch

Conch Fritters

Serves enough for a party

2–3 lbs. soft cleaned conch, chopped or minced	1 Tbs. lemon juice
	1 large onion
3 large garlic cloves	3 eggs
2 tsp. thyme	2 cups milk

Blend all of these except the conch until they're blended and pour this into a large mixing bowl.

Grind or finely chop the conch. (I use a blender: do just one conch at a time and stop the blender to push the conch down into the blade if you need to. Be careful not to purée the conch —it can happen fast. If some gets puréed, use it anyway, but the right texture of the conch is needed for this recipe along with the flavor.) Add the chopped conch to the mixture in the mixing bowl.

> 3 Tbs. minced parsley
> Crushed, dried red pepper, or minced jalapeño peppers
> 1 large sweet red pepper, minced
> 4 cups self-rising flour

Add the parsley, hot peppers, and sweet red pepper to the above conch mixture. Now add the flour one cup at a time, mixing well after each addition, till you have a very stiff batter. Cover the mixing bowl tightly with plastic film and refrigerate it for a couple of hours.

Heat oil to 350 degrees. Dip a long-handled spoon (an iced teaspoon works great) into the oil and then into the batter.

Slide the batter off the spoon into the hot oil with a rubber spatula or another spoon.

Fry these till they're light golden brown without crowding them in the pan, adjusting salt and pepper if needed.

Drain them on paper towels and keep them warm till you finish cooking.

These fritters are great served with cocktail sauce, tartar sauce, sweet-and-sour sauce, or a honey-mustard dip. If you have them on a buffet, be sure to replenish them frequently, because they need to be kept warm.

Mussels

Mussels in Cream-and-Herb Sauce

Serves 4

        2   Tbs. butter or margarine
       ½   lb. fresh mushrooms, thinly sliced
     6–8   shallots, minced
       ¼   cup white-wine vinegar
        2   lbs. fresh mussels, scrubbed and debearded
            Salt and pepper
       ¼   cup white wine
      1½   cups heavy whipping cream
        1   tsp. each parsley, chervil, freeze-dried chives,
                basil, mint

Melt the butter in a large skillet and cook the mushrooms while stirring till the juices have evaporated. Add the shallots and cook them for about a minute. Add the vinegar and cook till it's *almost* evaporated. Add the mussels, salt, and pepper, and then the white wine and boil this till the mussels open. Discard the unopened shells. Remove the opened mussels and set them aside, then boil the sauce till it's reduced to about half. Stir in the cream and boil it for about 5 minutes, or till the sauce is thick and creamy. Stir in the herbs and return the mussels to the sauce to reheat them.

Serve this with a good crusty bread to dip in the sauce, or white or yellow rice.

I came up with recipe once on the spur of the moment, and it has really gained a lot of good reviews.

Mussels With Curried Mayonnaise

Makes 48 individual

  48 mussels, scrubbed and debearded
    1 cup mayonnaise
2–3 tsp. curry powder

Boil the mussels in a large, covered stock pot on high heat till the shells open. Discard the unopened shells. Remove the good mussels from the shells and save half the shells.

Mix the mayonnaise and curry powder well together. Put each cooked mussel back into a half shell and and press these into crumpled aluminum foil on a serving plate. Drop a dollop of the curried mayonnaise on each mussel and garnish them with parsley and lemon slices.

Soups

and

Salads

Soups and Chowders

Basic Fish Stock or Court Bouillon

one 10–12-quart stockpot (stainless steel
     or enamel—not aluminum)
4 lbs. fish carcasses and heads
1 stick butter or margarine
1 large carrot, sliced
1 large celery stalk, sliced
1 large onion, sliced
½ cup chopped parsley
1 whole lemon, seeded and sliced
1 Tbs. dried whole thyme (fresh as possible—
    if yours is old, buy some new)
1 Tbs. coarse black pepper, freshly ground
1 or 2 garlic cloves, chopped (optional)
1 cup good, dry white wine
7 cups cold water
4 saffron threads (optional, and expensive,
    but what a difference!)

To get a really good stock you need the fish heads and bones—the best flavor comes from them. They also create a gelatin rather than a thin broth. And this stock will go a long way. You can use it for many different recipes.

Ask your fish market for fresh heads and bones. This might not cost you anything if you are a regular customer. And tell them you're making a stock and would like the gills removed. They may wish you hadn't asked that. But stand your ground. Tell them you'll be glad to pay. (Removing the gills isn't easy.) Then, ask the fish market to cut any large bones so they'll fit into your stockpot. And be ready to pay—you've just pushed as far as you can go! But, as I say, if you're a regular customer, they may just smile (teeth) and they may say "That's OK, no charge."

Anyway, however you get them, wash the fish heads and bones in water, trim off the fins if the fish market didn't and drain them in a colander over the sink.

Melt the butter in the stockpot. Add the carrots, celery, onion, parsley, lemon, thyme, pepper, and garlic, stir these well and cook till the vegetables start to steam, but don't fry them.

Add the prepared fish heads and bones, cover the stockpot, and cook these for about 15 minutes, stirring frequently, on low to medium heat. If the vegetables or fish start to get dry, don't cook them any longer.

Now add the white wine, cold water, and saffron if you're using it. Use enough water to cover the fish, then add about an inch extra. Bring this to a light "shimmer," but don't boil it. Place the lid on the pot loosely and cook this on low to medium heat for 30–45 minutes. Try not to stir the ingredients. If you think some fish or vegetables may be sticking in the pot, carefully lift them off the bottom of the pot and reduce the heat. As the foam comes to the top, skim it off with a spoon or skimmer.

Line a colander with about three layers of cheese cloth and set it over a large bowl. Carefully, pour the entire contents of the stockpot into the colander. With the back of a large wooden spoon, press the juices out of the fish and vegetables, without crushing them. Allow this stock to cool enough to refrigerate. Let the fat rise to the top and solidify, then remove and discard it. The stock in the bowl should be like gelatin. If so, perfect! If not, that's OK too. Cover it tightly and refrigerate it till you're ready to use it.

Now back to the fish heads and bones. After they've cooled sufficiently, very carefully pick the meat from the bones. You'll see lots of nice white meat across the top of the head, the cheeks, and the throat area around the mouth. Just look how much meat you've removed from those "bones!" This is delicious chilled and made into a fish salad or added to chowder, or even fish cakes.

It's such a waste to throw it away.

Please note that I haven't added salt. I do that when I've decided what to use the stock for.

Fish Bouillon from Basic Fish Stock

You'll need a Dutch oven or pot that holds at least 3 quarts. Put about 2 quarts of the fish stock in the pot and heat this slowly till the gelatin is dissolved. Then turn the heat to high and boil this till it's reduced to half.

Now you need a smaller, heavy pan. (Don't try to use a thin aluminum pan; it won't do the job.) Pour the reduced stock into the smaller pan and cook on medium heat till the stock is reduced to a syrupy consistency. The time depends on the basic stock, the thickness of the pot, and your patience. Try not to rush this process.

Pour this mixture into ice-cube trays, chill them, then cut them into cubes about tablespoon-size. Wrap these individually and freeze them.

This bouillon is much better than the type you can buy. The commercial varieties are laden with salt; usually it's the first ingredient on the label. What you make has no added salt. It can be used in just about anything you want concerning seafood: If a recipe calls for, say, clam juice, and you don't have any, just use water for the clam juice amount and a fish bouillon cube of your own.

From here on you can be very creative. There's no end to what you can do with the basic fish stock.

Cream of Sweet Red Pepper-And-Shrimp Soup

Serves 8

- 4 sweet red peppers, seeded and diced
- ½ lb. fresh spinach leaves, stems removed
- Juice of one fresh lemon
- 4 cups homemade or canned chicken broth
- 3 large shallots, chopped
- 1 tsp. green onions, finely chopped
- 1 tsp. salt
- ½ tsp. white pepper
- 1 lb. fresh shrimp, peeled, deveined, and coarsely chopped

ROUX:

- 3 Tbs. butter
- 3 Tbs. flour
- ½–1 cup half-and-half

Combine the peppers, spinach, and lemon juice in a bowl. Heat the broth in a medium saucepan till it simmers, add the peppers and spinach mixture, shallots, onions, salt, and pepper, cover, and let it simmer for 30 minutes.

Transfer the pepper-and-spinach mixture into a blender, with enough liquid to cover, and purée till completely smooth. Reserve the rest of the liquid.

For the roux, melt butter in a medium-size saucepan, stir in the flour, and cook till it's light golden brown. Add the reserved liquid and purée this in the blender. Back in the pan, bring this to a boil, reduce the heat and add the shrimp, and simmer about 8 minutes, stirring frequently.

Remove from the heat and let it cool slightly. Add the half-and-half and strain through a fine sieve. Return only the shrimp to the soup, discarding the pulp in the sieve.

If the soup is too thick, thin it with additional chicken broth, not half-and-half.

Quick Shrimp Soup

Makes about 8 bowls

  3 cups canned or homemade chicken broth
  3 cups milk
  1 tsp. dill weed
  ¼ cup tomato paste
  3 Tbs. fresh parsley, chopped
  ¼ cup heavy whipping cream
  1 lb. cooked shrimp, peeled, deveined, and
      coarsely chopped
  2 Tbs. freshly squeezed lemon juice
Freshly ground pepper
Paprika for garnish
  ½ cup all-purpose flour
Butter or margarine

First make the roux: Brown the flour in the butter and stir till it's thick. In a large (6- to 7-quart-size) pot, combine the broth, milk, dill weed, tomato paste, and parsley. Whisk this well and bring it to a boil, stirring frequently. Reduce the heat and let it simmer for about 10 minutes. Stir in the cream and the shrimp and immediately add the roux, stirring constantly. Remove this from the heat and add the fresh lemon juice.

I don't add salt unless it really needs it. Remember that most chicken broths are salted.

Add just enough of the roux to thicken the soup to your liking. I find the above amount just right for me; you may not want to use it all.

Clam Chowder, Creamy Style

Makes about 18 bowls

- 2 sticks butter or margarine
- ½ cup chopped onion
- ½ cup chopped celery
- one 8-oz. bottle clam juice
- 3 cups potatoes, peeled and diced
- 1 gallon milk
- 1 lb. frozen, diced clams
- 2 Tbs. chopped fresh or dehydrated parsley
- 2 Tbs. seafood seasoning
- 2 Tbs. whole thyme
- Salt and pepper

ROUX:

- 2 sticks butter or margarine
- 1 cup all-purpose flour

In a large stockpot or soup pot, melt the two sticks of butter, add the onions and celery, and cook till they're transparent. Add the clam juice and potatoes and cook till the potatoes are about half-done.

Warm the milk in another pan, pour it into the stockpot, and bring this to a simmer, but don't boil it.

In the meantime, make the roux: Melt the butter in a small saucepan and gradually add the flour while stirring till the mixture resembles the thickness of honey. I find that the amount of flour will vary with the different brands of butters or margarines. Cook this over very low heat just a little bit, to reduce the flour taste. Pour the roux slowly into the chowder while stirring, on low heat.

Now it's time to add the clams, parsley, and seasonings. Stir these well and turn off the heat.

This may sound like a lot of chowder. Believe me it isn't, unless you're cooking for two. And even then the left overs have never gone to waste in my house. It will keep for about three days. Three days, that is, if you handle the hot chowder properly. Here's how:

Cool it to room temperature, or close, and pour it into a container with a tight-fitting lid. Do **not** put the lid on now. Put the chowder in the refrigerator. When it's **cold**, put the lid on tightly. When you're ready for some chowder take out only the amount that you plan to eat and replace the lid.

Manhattan Clam Chowder

Makes about 6 large bowls

- 1½ cups water
- two 16-oz. cans whole tomatoes, chopped (keep the juice or sauce)
- ½ cup chopped celery
- ½ cup sweet green pepper, chopped
- 2 Tbs. butter or margarine
- 1½ cups clam juice
- 2 Tbs. Worcestershire sauce
- ½ cup onions, chopped
- 1 tsp. each basil, thyme, salt, and pepper
- 2 or more bay leaves

Cook all of the above in a large pot for 30–45 minutes. Then add 2 cups of peeled and diced white potatoes and cook these till the potatoes are nearly done. Then add 1-1/2 cups of fresh, chopped clams.

Turn the heat off and leave the pot on the burner for about 5–10 minutes. This allows the clams to cook just right—not tough.

I like to add a box of frozen peas or cut green beans once in a while to stretch the servings for unexpected guests. I also like to add a small amount of roux to thicken the chowder. This is not a traditional Manhattan-style clam chowder, but my own version.

Easy New England-Style Clam Chowder

Serves about 6

- 3 small cans minced clams or 2 cans whole baby clams
- 1 can cream-of-mushroom soup
- 1 small can corn
- 1 can sliced or diced potatoes
- 2–3 pints half-and-half

Mix all the above ingredients and cook slowly on low heat. Add a touch of white wine if you like, and salt and white pepper to taste.

Fish Chowder Florentine

Serves 8-10

¼ cup chopped salt-pork
¼ cup onion, chopped
¼ cup celery, chopped
2 cups potatoes, diced
one 14½-oz. can chicken broth
1 lb. fish fillets, cut into 1-inch cubes
3 cups milk
3–4 Tbs. flour
1 cup heavy whipping cream
one 10-oz. pkg. frozen chopped spinach, cooked

Brown the salt-pork in a large pot or Dutch oven. Remove the pork, leaving at least 4 tablespoons of the drippings in the oven. Add to this the onion, celery, and potatoes and cook these till the onion is transparent and the celery is tender. Add the chicken broth, cover, and cook this till the potatoes are tender. Add the fish and 2-1/2 cups of the milk. Bring this to a boil, then reduce the heat and let it simmer for about 2–4 minutes. Shake the remaining cold milk and the flour together, stir this into the chowder very gently and cook till it's bubbly. Add the cream, spinach, salt, and pepper to taste and heat till it's hot but don't let it boil.

You can add any other kind of seafood you like and call this seafood chowder florentine. Shrimp, clams, oysters, etc., are all good together with this fish.

I add a dash of thyme or a couple of dashes of hot sauce, and sometimes a couple tablespoons of minced sweet red pepper or diced pimientos. The peppers are more for color than taste.

Whether you add anything or not, this is a great chowder.

Curried Shrimp-Veggie Chowder

Serves 6-8

- 3½ cups chicken broth
- ¼ cup white rice
- one 10-oz. pkg. frozen chopped broccoli
- 1 cup carrots, chopped
- 1½ cups milk
- 4 Tbs. butter or margarine
- 4 Tbs. all-purpose flour
- 1 tsp. curry powder
- 1 lb. shrimp, peeled, deveined, and chopped

Stir the chicken broth and rice together in a 4-quart saucepan, bring this to a boil, reduce the heat, cover and let it simmer for 10 minutes. Stir in the broccoli and carrots, return this to a boil, then reduce the heat and let it simmer for 8–10 minutes, or till the vegetables and rice are tender. Add the milk slowly and let it simmer till it's hot but don't let it boil.

Melt the butter or margarine in a small saucepan or skillet, add the flour and mix well, then add the curry powder.

Add the chopped shrimp to the hot chowder and cook this for a few minutes, being very careful not to let it boil.

When the shrimp are done, add the butter, flour, and curry mixture, stirring constantly, and heat this till it's thick. Add salt and pepper to taste.

This chowder is rather heavy and rich for an appetizer, so I prefer to serve it as a main course with garlic toast or bread. It's also good with a dollop of sour cream on top and sprinkled with fresh, sliced green onions.

Conch Chowder

Serves 6 qts.

- **2–3 lbs. frozen conch (preferably queen conch), thawed and cleaned**
- **8 Tbs. butter or margarine**
- **6–8 carrots, chopped**
- **6–8 celery stalks, chopped**
- **2 large onions, chopped**
- **6–8 garlic cloves, chopped**

Chop the conch in a processor or blender. Chop them one at a time and use a little water if they stick.

Sauté the rest of the above ingredients (no conch) in the butter in a 6-quart (at least) stockpot till the onions are transparent.

- **2 large cans tomato purée**
- **2 Tbs. fresh or dried whole thyme**
- **Jalapeño peppers to taste**
- **5 lbs. potatoes, cooked, peeled, and diced**
- **1 whole lemon**

Add the conch, tomato purée, thyme and enough water to make the stockpot 3/4 full. Bring this to a boil, stirring frequently. Reduce the heat and let this simmer covered for about an hour. In the last 10 minutes of cooking time, add coarsley chopped Jalapeño peppers — use discretion, as the more you use the hotter it tastes — and the cooked potatoes. Then add the lemon, rind and all, but without the seeds. Bring this to a boil, stirring frequently, then let it simmer for 10–12 minutes.

(continued next page)

8 Tbs. butter or margarine, melted
½ cup all-purpose flour
1 sweet red pepper, diced
1 sweet green pepper, diced
3—4 whole bay leaves
1 half-bunch fresh parsley
Salt and pepper
Sherry

Whisk the butter and the flour together and pour this into the chowder while stirring. Be sure to scrape the bottom so nothing sticks or burns. Stir in the peppers, bay leaves, and parsley. Turn off the heat and add salt and pepper to taste.

Pour a shot of sherry into each soup bowl, ladle in the chowder, and sprinkle it with a few thinly sliced, pitted black olives. Serve this with a good crusty bread.

Open your doors and windows while cooking this and all your neighbors from within 5 blocks will be at your door. A man from Wisconsin once told me, "Bottle that aroma, Rose, and you'll make a fortune." Never quite figured out how, though.

Seafood Gumbo

Makes 6-8 large bowls

- ½ cup all-purpose flour
- ½ cup oil
- 2 cups onion, chopped
- 1 cup green pepper, chopped
- 5 garlic cloves, chopped (or less, to your taste)
- 6 cups hot water
- one 10-oz. package frozen okra, thawed
- 2 tsp. filé powder
- 1 bay leaf
- 1 lb. fresh frozen shrimp, peeled and deveined
- ½ lb. crabmeat

Cook the flour and oil in a heavy, 4-quart dutch oven, on medium heat. Stir this often till it's dark reddish-brown. This can take anywhere from 10 minutes to half an hour. It has to be done with patience. If the roux gets too dark, throw it out and start over.

Add the onion, green pepper, and garlic and cook these while stirring on medium heat till the vegetables are tender. Stir in the hot water, okra, filé powder, and bay leaf, season to taste with salt, and bring this to a boil. Reduce the heat and let it simmer covered for about an hour.

Add the seafood and let it simmer uncovered till the shrimp turn pink. Remove the bay leaf and serve the gumbo over rice.

Stews and Casseroles

Shrimp-Veggie Casserole

Serves 4-6

- ½ cup onion, minced
- ½ cup mayonnaise
- ½ can condensed cream-of-shrimp soup, undiluted
- ½ tsp. garlic powder or fresh minced garlic
- 1 can mixed vegetables, well drained
- 4 ounces cheddar or Swiss cheese, grated
- ½ cup cooked shrimp
- ¼ cup parsley, minced
- ½ cup Italian-seasoned bread crumbs
- 2 Tbs. melted butter or margarine
- Salt and white pepper

Combine all of these except the bread crumbs and melted butter and put this mixture into a greased 1-1/2-quart casserole.

Mix the bread crumbs and melted butter, sprinkle this over the casserole, and bake it at 350 degrees for 20–25 minutes, or till the crumbs are light golden brown and the casserole is bubbly around the edges.

I'm not usually too keen on casseroles, but this combination came out once when I needed a "heat and eat" item. Since then, I've made at least a ton of it. The leftovers are delicious, too.

Shrimp-and-Asparagus Casserole

Serves 6

- 1 lb. small or medium shrimp, peeled and deveined
- ¼ cup minced celery
- ¼ cup minced onion
- 1 pkg. frozen asparagus, cooked
- 1 can cream-of-mushroom soup, undiluted
- 2 Tbs. grated Parmesan cheese
- ¼ cup. pkg. bread crumbs
- 3 Tbs. melted butter or margarine

Boil a little water in a medium-size saucepan and then add the shrimp. When the water boils again, remove the shrimp and then drain well.

Lay the shimp, celery, onion, asparagus, and soup in layers in a buttered 2-to-3-quart casserole. Spread a mixture of the cheese, crumbs, and melted butter on top and bake it at 350 degrees till it's bubbly and the crumb topping has browned nicely.

This is a very quick casserole to put together. I sometimes make it before going to work in the morning. I make the casserole up to the topping and refrigerate it. When I get home I turn the oven on, and slide it into the oven. It takes about 15 minutes longer to bake when it has to be refrigerated like this.

Shrimp, Crabmeat and Broccoli Casserole

Serves 4-6

- one 10-oz. pkg. frozen chopped broccoli
- ½ lb. crabmeat (any kind)
- 1 lb. small or medium shrimp, peeled, deveined and cooked
- ½ pint sour cream
- ¼ cup chili sauce
- ¼ cup chopped onion
- 1 cup grated cheddar cheese
- 1 Tbs. lemon juice

Cook and drain the broccoli, mix it with the rest of the ingredients and bake this in a shallow well-buttered casserole at 350 degrees for 20–25 minutes, till the cheese is melted and the top is light golden brown.

This is excellent for a quick dinner with a minimum of time and work. And, of course, you can vary the seafood. Maybe you have an extra lobster tail from last night's dinner; chop it up and add it to the casserole.

Fast-and-Easy
Broccoli-and-Seafood Casserole

Serves 6

- two 10-oz. pkgs. frozen broccoli spears, cooked
- 1 cup lobster meat, cooked
- ½ lb. medium or large shrimp, peeled, deveined, and cooked
- 3 hard-boiled eggs, sliced
- 2 envelopes Hollandaise sauce

(continued next page)

Fast-and-Easy Broccoli-and-Seafood Casserole
(Continued from previous page)

Milk (for the Hollandaise)
 - **½ cup sour cream**
 - **1 cup bread crumbs**
 - **3 Tbs. grated Parmesan cheese**
 - **2 Tbs. butter or margarine, melted**

Arrange the broccoli, lobster, and shrimp in layers in a buttered rectangular baking dish at least 2 inches deep, and lay the eggs on top.

Prepare the Hollandaise sauce according to the directions, using the milk. When you're finished cooking it, add the sour cream and spoon this over the casserole. Mix the bread crumbs, Parmesan cheese, and melted butter, sprinkle this on top and bake it at 350 degrees for 20–25 minutes, till it's bubbly and hot.

Seafood Stew, My Way

Serves 8-10

- ½ lb. sausage, ground and processed with bacon
- ¼ lb. sliced bacon, ground or chopped in processor
- 2 Tbs. olive oil
- ½ cup onion, chopped
- ½ cup celery, coarsely chopped
- ½ cup green pepper, chopped
- one 10-oz. pkg. frozen okra, thawed
- 2 cups fish stock
- 2 cups tomato sauce
- 2 cups chili sauce
- 1 Tbs. lemon juice
- 1 tsp. filé powder
- Salt and pepper
- ½ lb. shucked clams, chopped
- ½ lb. grouper or any lean white fish, cubed
- ½ lb. shrimp, whole, peeled, deveined, with tails off

Cook the sausage and bacon in a skillet, drain them and set them aside.

In a large stockpot on medium high heat sauté the onion, celery, and green pepper, in the olive oil till the vegetables are soft but not brown. Stir in the sausage and bacon, reduce the heat to low, and cook this for 2 minutes.

Add the okra to the stockpot and cook it briefly, then add the stock, tomato sauce, chili sauce, lemon juice, filé powder, and salt to taste, and continue cooking this on low heat for 12–15 minutes, stirring occasionally.

Add the seafood and cook till they're done, 3–5 minutes, depending on their size.

Serve this with a hot, crusty, French garlic bread. Believe me, your dinner guests will clean their bowls.

Seafood Paella

Serves 6-8

This is not an authentic Spanish-style paella, but my own seafood version. The seafood can be whatever is available—the more seafood, the more attractive and delicious. This is definitely "company fare."

½ cup extra-virgin olive oil
1 medium-size onion, chopped
8–10 garlic cloves, crushed
1 medium-size sweet red pepper, chopped
3 cups converted rice
3 cups canned chicken broth
2½ cups clam juice
4 small bay leaves
1 tsp. saffron threads, steeped in 2 Tbs. hot
     water and crushed
one 10-oz. pkg. frozen peas, rinsed and thawed
   Salt and freshly ground pepper
1 lb. medium or large shrimp, peeled and
     deveined, with tails off
4 lobster tails, about 6-oz. each, removed from
     shell and split lengthwise
1 lb. firm white fish such as grouper, cod,
     haddock, cut into 1-inch cubes
16 littleneck clams, cleaned
16 mussels, scrubbed and debearded
8 shucked oysters
8 medium stone-crab claws (if available)

Heat a quarter-cup of the olive oil in a large skillet till a haze forms over the top, then add the onions, garlic, and sweet red pepper and cook these on medium heat till they're softened, about 5 minutes. Stir in the rice and cook while stirring, till it's translucent. Add the chicken broth, clam juice, bay leaves, and the saffron liquid, bring this to a boil, then reduce the heat to low and cook this, stirring occasionally, till the rice is tender on the outside but still chewy in the center. Stir in the peas, salt, and pepper and transfer the mixture to a 15-inch paella pan or a large oven-proof skillet.

Cook the shrimp, lobster, and fish separately in the other quarter-cup of olive oil. Push the shrimp, fish, clams, oysters, and crab (shellfish hinge-side down) into the rice, and lay the lobster tails on top.

Bake the paella for 30 minutes or till the rice is tender and the clams and mussels are open. Discard any unopened ones. Remove this from the oven and cover it loosely with foil for 10 minutes. Garnish it with parsley and lemon wedges, and serve it directly from the pan.

Salads

Smoked-Fish Salad

Makes 8

- ½ cup vegetable oil
- 3 Tbs. Dijon mustard
- 2 Tbs. red wine vinegar
- 1 lb. smoked fish

Fresh spinach, rinsed, patted dry, with stems removed

- 2 large, ripe, firm tomatoes, sliced
- 1 lb. Mozzarella cheese, sliced

Whisk the oil, mustard, and vinegar together till well mixed and set this aside.

Slice or break the fish into pieces. Line a large platter with the spinach leaves and arrange the smoked fish, tomato, and cheese on this. Pour some of the vinegar mixture over the salad and use the rest at the table.

This salad is good served as an appetizer. It's a good idea to prepare the platter about half an hour before you're ready to serve it. It looks nice served with fish, tomatoes, and cheese on a platter surrounding a bowl of the extra dressing in the middle.

Curried-Fish Salad

Serves 4 large, 8 small

- 2   cups cold, cooked fish (any kind)
- 1   small onion, minced
- 1   garlic clove, minced
- 1   tsp. dry mustard
- ¼   cup celery, finely minced, or 1 Tbs. celery seed
- 1   Tbs. lemon juice
- ¼   cup fresh minced or dehydrated parsley
- 1   Tbs. fresh curry powder, or to taste
-    Salt and white pepper
-    Mayonnaise to moisten

Mix all of these except the mayonnaise. Refrigerate for about an hour, then add the mayonnaise to moisten. Keep this in the refrigerator till you're ready to serve it. The salad will become slightly pale yellow in appearence. This is because of the curry.

If you want a tangier flavor, add more dry mustard or even a hot pepper sauce.

Serve it on lettuce leaves with hard-boiled egg wedges, tomatoes, and crackers.

Or slice a "V" out of a sub roll and pull it apart slightly. Add a small amount of shredded lettuce, then the fish salad and garnish it with chopped hard-boiled eggs. Replace the "V" on the roll.

Or, core and cut a tomato into wedges, without cutting through it. Stuff this with the fish salad and set it on a bed of lettuce topped with chopped egg.

This is a recipe you can use your imagination with.

I must have made a ton of this salad in the last six years and have got lots of compliments for it.

Seafood Antipasto

Serves about 10

- 1 lb. cold, poached fish (swordfish, tuna, salmon, or cod)
- 1 jar marinated artichoke hearts, split
- 1 cup celery, diagonally sliced
- 1 can chickpeas, rinsed and drained well
- 4–6 hard-boiled eggs, cut into wedges
- 1 lb. large shrimp, peeled, deveined, cooked, and chilled
- 1 can pitted black olives, rinsed and drained well
- ½ lb. of string Mozzarella cheeese, cut into bite-size pieces
- 2–4 kiwi fruits, peeled and sliced
- 1 or 2 lemons, sliced
- About 1 pint homemade Italian dressing, or a good commercial one

Arrange all of these ingredients on a platter, lettuce-lined or plain, and serve immediately. Drizzle some dressing over it and use the rest at the table.

This really makes a beautiful platter, and the combination of flavors is great. Of course, you can use any other kind of ingredient you like. I've even used mustard and oil-packed sardines.

I had this for some friends recently, and one of them kept pushing the fish aside. When I asked him why, he said he had never heard of cold fish and Italian dressing and just didn't think the two went together. I asked him how he knew if he had never tried it.

He did try it, and his wife tells me that every time they have fish now, some has to be put back in the refrigerator to get cold so he can have an antipasto the next night.

Shrimp Salad with Caper Vinaigrette

Makes 3

- ½ cup olive oil
- ¼ cup white-wine vinegar
- 1 Tbs. lemon juice
- ½ tsp. sugar

- 3 Tbs. capers, rinsed, drained, and chopped
- Salt and freshly ground pepper
- 1 cup shrimp, peeled, deveined, cooked, and coarsely chopped
- 2 Tbs. minced onion
- 1 small tomato, peeled, seeded, and cubed
- ½ small avocado, peeled, seeded, and cubed
- 2 tsp. fresh minced parsley
- Crisp lettuce leaves (can be thinly sliced)

Whisk together the olive oil, wine vinegar, lemon juice, sugar, salt, and pepper. Add the capers, shrimp, and onion and toss these lightly, then refrigerate it for about 15 minutes before adding the tomato, avocado, and parsley. Toss this, and serve it on three lettuce-lined salad plates.

This makes a delicious cold-luncheon plate. Just don't make it too far in advance. Add bread sticks, crackers, or Melba toast.

Shrimp, Avocado, and Macadamia-Nut Salad

Makes 6

- ½ cup salad oil
- ½ cup white vinegar
- 1 large garlic clove, finely minced and crushed
- Salt and pepper
- 1 lb. shrimp, peeled, deveined, cooked, and well-chilled
- 1 large or 2 medium-size avocados
- ¼ cup macadamia nuts, coarsely chopped

In a blender, thoroughly blend the oil, vinegar, and garlic, add salt and pepper to taste, and pour this into a large bowl.

If the shrimp are larger than bite-size, cut them up, then add them to the vinegar mixture (vinaigrette). Peel the avocado, cut them into bite-size pieces, and add them to the shrimp and vinaigrette and toss this well to coat everything. Refrigerate it for about 4 hours before serving it.

Serve this in a lettuce-lined bowl sprinkled with chopped macadamia nuts.

I could eat avocados every day of my life and never tire of them. And this combination is excellent; the nuts add just enough crunch to set off the softness of the avocado.

Dilled Florida Shrimp and Pasta Salad

Serves 8

DILLED LEMON DRESSING:
- 1 cup fresh parsley leaves
- 6 large shallots
- 2 large garlic cloves
- 2/3 cup oil
- 6 Tbs. fresh dill weed or 3 Tbs. dried
- 1/2 cup fresh lemon juice
- Salt and pepper

- 2 lbs. Florida shrimp
- 1/4 cup oil
- 1 box frozen snow-peas
- one 8-oz. can whole water chestnuts, drained and sliced
- 1 large or 2 small sweet red peppers, cut into thin strips
- 1 lb. spaghetti
- 2 quarts water

Put half the parsley leaves and all of the shallots, garlic, oil, dill weed, lemon juice, salt, and pepper in a blender and blend till smooth.

Cook the spaghetti just till it's "al dente": firm but not too done.

Peel and devein the shrimp and stir-fry them in oil, about half a pound at a time, till they're done. Don't overcook them. Then split the shrimp in half, lengthwise, add half the dill dressing to the skillet, and heat for about 2 minutes.

Put the drained spaghetti in a glass or ceramic bowl, add the water chestnuts and pepper strips, pour in the dilled dressing from the blender, and toss this carefully.

Cook the peas, plunge them into ice-cold water, drain well, pat them dry, and add them to the pasta, along with the shrimp and dressing. Toss this well and cool it to room temperature before serving it.

Shrimp Salad--My Special #1

Makes 4-6

- 2 cups shrimp, cooked and chopped
- 1 small can unsweetened crushed pineapple, well-drained
- 1 Tbs. fresh horseradish
- 1 Tbs. white pepper or freshly ground black pepper
- 2 Tbs. fresh lemon juice
- 2 Tbs. fresh minced parsley, or dehydrated or freeze-dried chives

Mayonnaise (*not* salad dressing)

Mix all of these with just enough mayonnaise to moisten it and hold it together nicely and serve this on a bed of lettuce with crackers.

This is also great on a sub roll. Cut a "V" out of a 6-inch roll, line the cavity with a little finely chopped lettuce, add the shrimp salad, and pop the "V" back in.

Crabmeat Salad

Makes 6

½ lb. fresh asparagus spears

2 cups crabmeat (Alaskan king crab, stone crab, blue crab, or imitation)

3 medium-size tomatoes, peeled, seeded, and chopped

3 egg yolks

1 Tbs. lemon juice

1 Tbs. freeze-dried chives

2 tsp. Dijon mustard

1 tsp. grated lemon peel

1 Tbs. tarragon vinegar

1 cup olive oil

6 Tbs. safflower oil

2 Tbs. pimiento, rinsed, drained, and chopped

Boil the asparagus spears for about 3 minutes, till they're crisp and tender. Plunge them into ice water, drain and dry them, and cut the tips diagonally into half-inch pieces. Gently toss the crabmeat, asparagus, and tomatoes together.

Combine the egg yolks, lemon juice, chives, mustard, lemon peel, and tarragon vinegar in a processor or blender. With the machine running, gradually add the olive oil and vegetable oil in a slow, steady stream and mix this till it's thick and creamy.

Pour this dressing over the crabmeat mixture and toss it gently, then cover it and refrigerate it for about 2 hours.

Serve this as a salad course or a luncheon plate, with a dollop of sour cream with seeded and diced cucumbers mixed in, and with crackers. It's very refreshing.

I like to stuff blue-crab shells with this salad if I have them. I also have some nice crab-shaped glass dishes that I use, or I just put the salad on a bed of lettuce and garnish it with hard-boiled eggs.

Crabmeat-and-Artichoke Salad

Makes 4 large, or 6 small salads

- 1 cup fresh crabmeat (lump, backfin, special, claw, or canned)
- 1 large can artichoke hearts, drained and chopped
- 3 hard-boiled eggs, chopped
- ¼ cup fresh mushrooms, thinly sliced
- ½ cup mayonnaise
- 2 Tbs. dry sherry
- 2 Tbs. chopped green onions or freeze-dried chives or parsley
- Salt and pepper

Toss all these lightly together and refrigerate this till serving time. Serve it on a bed of lettuce with a lemon wedge.

Sauces

For Fish
as Toppings

Tartar Sauce

Makes 1¼ cup
- 1 cup mayonnaise
- 3 Tbs. sweet-pickle relish
- 1 Tbs. minced onion
- 2 Tbs. lemon juice
- 1 Tbs. Worcestershire sauce

Mix these and refrigerate.

If you like a little more "bite", add a dash or two of Tabasco sauce or any good hot sauce, or even a few crushed red peppers. But use these with caution! For a little more color add about a tablespoon of fresh minced or dehydrated parsley or even a few chives.

The following is a good sauce for fish instead of the traditional tartar sauce.

Makes about 1¼ cup
- 1 cup mayonnaise
- 2 Tbs. tomato paste
- 2–3 Tbs. freeze-dried chives
- ¼ tsp. dried whole chevril
- ¼ tsp. dried whole tarragon
- 1 dash garlic powder

Stir these well and refrigerate for about an hour for the flavors to blend.

Jalapeño-Pepper Sauce

Makes about 1 cup

- 1 cup mayonnaise
- 5 Jalapeño peppers, or to taste
- 1 Tbs. fresh parsley, minced
- 1 Tbs. lemon juice
- 1 Tbs. minced pimiento
- 1 Tbs. black olives, finely minced

Mix all these and refrigerate for the flavors to blend. Use the jalapeños sparingly. This makes a great tartar sauce, if you don't get it too hot. It's especially good with pan-fried or deep-fried oysters.

Cocktail Sauce

Makes about 1 cup

- ½ cup chili sauce
- 2 Tbs. prepared horseradish
- 2 Tbs. sweet-pickle relish
- 1 Tbs. Worcestershire sauce
- 1 garlic clove, finely minced
- 1 Tbs. lemon juice
- 1 Tbs. fresh parsley, minced

Mix these and refrigerate for several hours for the flavors to blend.

Cucumber-Dill Sauce

Makes about 1 cup
- 8 oz. sour cream
- 1 medium cucumber, peeled, seeded, and finely chopped
- 1 tsp. dill weed
- 1 tsp. sugar

Mix and salt to taste.

Garlic Sauce

Makes about ½ cup
- 2–4 garlic cloves, minced, to taste
- ¼ cup bread crumbs
- 1 Tbs. olive oil
- 1 Tbs. wine vinegar
- 1 chopped parsley

Fish bouillon or court bouillon or chicken broth

Mash the garlic and bread crumbs into a paste, mix in the oil, stir in the vinegar and parsley, then add bouillon a little at a time till the paste is of a pouring consistency.

Garlic-Oil Sauce

Makes about 1 cup

  2 egg yolks
  3 Tbs. lemon juice
5–8 garlic cloves, to taste
     Salt and pepper
  ¼ cup olive oil
  ½ cup vegetable oil

At high speed, blend the egg yolks, lemon juice, garlic, salt, pepper, and olive oil till they're well blended. With the blender running pour the salad oil into the small opening in a slow steady stream. Refrigerate this till you're ready to use it. This is great on any seafood, and especially on fish, shrimp, or scallops.

Bechamel Sauce

Makes 2 cups

  4 Tbs. butter or margarine
  4 Tbs. flour
1½ cups half-and-half
  1 cup dry white wine, or less
  ¼ cup fresh minced parsley
  ¼ cup Parmesan cheese, freshly grated
     Salt and pepper

Melt the butter in a heavy saucepan, add the flour, and stir it to a smooth paste. Gradually add the half-and-half while stirring till it's thick. Stir in just enough wine to thicken the sauce down a bit, but not too much, then remove this from the heat and add the parsley, grated cheese, salt, and pepper. Add more wine if the sauce is still a little too thick.

Lemon-Pepper Sauce

Makes about 2 cups

   1 cup oil
  ¼ cup lemon juice
  ¼ cup red wine vinegar
  2 Tbs. Dijon mustard
  4 garlic cloves
Salt and pepper
  2 Tbs. sliced green onions, with some of the green
  ½ cup sweet red pepper, minced

Blend all these except the onions and red peppers, till the garlic is puréed, then stir in the onions and peppers without blending further.

This is a good, tangy sauce for fish. It doesn't require much.

I've also used it to marinate shrimp before grilling or broiling. And it's best of all for marinating fresh tuna steaks before grilling.

Dilled Horseradish Sauce

Makes about 1 cup

one 3-oz. pkg. cream cheese, softened
  ½ cup sour cream
  2 Tbs. horseradish
  1 tsp. sugar
  ½ tsp. dried dillweed

Beat these together and refrigerate it for several hours.

Shrimp-and-Scallop Sauce

For 2 lbs. fish

- 1¼ sticks unsalted butter
- 4 small shallots, minced
- ½ lb. fresh sea scallops, sliced, not cooked
- 1 cup dry white wine
- Salt and pepper
- 2 cups heavy cream
- 15 large fresh mushrooms, cleaned and sliced
- ½ lb. fresh shrimp, cooked, peeled, and deveined

Melt two tablespoons of the butter in a large skillet, add the shallots, wine, salt and pepper and cook them for 2–3 minutes, then add the scallops and cook the remaining liquid on medium heat till it's reduced to half. Lower the heat again, add the cream, and cook while stirring till it's thick.

Using a whisk, add 6 tablespoons of the butter one tablespoon at a time, then remove the sauce from the heat and set it aside, keeping it warm.

Melt the remaining butter in a skillet on medium heat, add the mushrooms and sauté them till they're cooked and the juices have evaporated. Blend the mushrooms, scallops, and shrimp into the sauce and heat it but don't let it boil.

Serve over broiled or poached fish of any kind or added to cooked croquettes or over freshly baked crepes. No matter what you serve it with, it has to be a winner.

Cointreau-and-Pistachio Sauce

Makes about ¾ cup

    2 Tbs. butter or margarine
    ½ cup pistachio nuts, shelled, with outer skin
       removed
    ¼ cup Cointreau liqueur

Sauté the nuts in the butter on medium-high heat for about 2 minutes, then stir in the Cointreau and remove it from the heat.

What a suprise with this combination—so good on baked or broiled fish.

Green Onion-Mustard Sauce

Makes about 3 cups

    1 bunch fresh green onions, thinly sliced
    1 egg
    1 Tbs. wine vinegar
    1 Tbs. black pepper, freshly ground
    2 Tbs. Dijon mustard
    Salt and pepper
    2 cups olive oil

Blend all these except the olive oil, then run the blender on slow while slowly pouring in the olive oil till the mixture becomes thick like mayonnaise.

This is excellent to use with fish instead of tartar sauce, or as a dip for shrimp.

Also, after baking or broiling fish, you can spread a thin layer of this over them and broil for about 2 more minutes.

Honey-Mustard Sauce

Makes about 1 cup

 ½ cup white wine vinegar
 2 Tbs. fresh lemon juice
 2 tsp. freeze-dried chives
 2 tsp. minced onion
 2 tsp. Dijon mustard
 2 tsp. honey
 ¼–½ cup safflower oil
 Salt and pepper

Blend all these except the safflower oil, then mix in the blender on low while slowly pouring in the oil. Add more oil if needed.

This is good on baked or broiled fish. I've also used it as a salad dressing. If it's too sweet for you, just use less honey.

Wine-Cream Sauce

Makes about 1¾ cups

 2 Tbs. butter or margarine
 2 Tbs. flour
 ¼ tsp. salt
 1 cup light cream
 1 egg yolk, slightly beaten
 ¼ cup dry white wine
 2 Tbs. chopped pimiento
 2 Tbs. capers, well drained

In a small saucepan blend the flour and salt into the melted butter, add the cream all at once, and cook this while stirring till it's thick and bubbly. Stir about half this mixture into the egg yolk, then back into the remaining mixture, and cook while stirring for 1–2 minutes longer. Now stir in the wine, pimiento, and capers, and heat it further but don't let it boil.

Mustard-Cream Sauce

Makes about 1 cup

- ⅔ cup milk
- 4 tsp. flour
- ¼ tsp. dry mustard
- ¼ tsp. onion salt
- Dash of pepper
- ⅓ cup sour cream

Shake the milk, flour, mustard, onion salt, and pepper in a jar with a screw-top lid till they're well blended and smooth. Cook this mixture in a saucepan while stirring till it's thick and bubbly, then gradually blend it into the sour cream, before returning it to the saucepan and heating it through. Don't let it boil.

Shallot-Cream Sauce

Makes about 1 cup

- 4 Tbs. unsalted butter
- 4–6 medium shallots, sliced thinly
- 2 Tbs. all-purpose flour
- ½ cup dry white wine
- ½ cup heavy whipping cream
- Salt, pepper, and chopped fresh parsley for garnish

In a skillet, sauté the shallots in the butter till they're tender, then remove them, leaving the butter in the skillet, and whisk the flour into the butter. Add more butter if the mixture seems too dry. Gradually whisk the wine into the skillet and bring this to a boil, then cook while stirring till the liquid is reduced to half. Now add the cream and cook it for 2 more minutes.

Olive-Cream Sauce

Makes about 2½–3 cups

         2 Tbs. butter or margarine
         2 Tbs. dry sherry
         ¼ cup minced onion
         ¼ cup canned mushrooms, chopped
         ½ cup sliced green olives with pimientos
         ½ cup sliced black olives, whole and seedless
         1 small garlic clove, crushed or ½ tsp. minced
                garlic packed in oil
      1–2 dashes Worcestershire sauce
         1 cup sour cream

   Heat the butter, sherry, onions, and mushrooms just till they're hot. Add the olives, garlic, and Worcestershire sauce and heat this just till it's warm.
   This is good with any kind of fish, or with shrimp.

For Cooking

Pesto

Makes about 2 cups

I know what you're thinking—"What's a pesto sauce doing in a seafood cookbook?" But wait and see what can be done!

> 2 cups fresh basil leaves, packed tightly
> 1 garlic clove
> ¼ tsp. salt
> 1 cup olive oil
> ½ cup pine (pignoli) nuts
> Freshly ground pepper

First, rinse and pat-dry the basil leaves, then blend everything well and refrigerate it in a glass or a non-metal jar with a tight-fitting lid. This pesto will keep in the refrigerator for about 2 weeks. If you can't find pine nuts, English walnuts will work. Use about twice as much.

Now, try these...

Pesto-Broiled Halibut

Serves 2–3

> 1 lb. halibut steaks
> 2 Tbs. pesto sauce

Spread the sauce on both sides of the steaks and refrigerate them for about an hour before broiling or grilling. Cook the steaks about 4 inches from the heat, no closer.

You can also bake or broil the steaks with just butter or margarine and pat a teaspoon or so on top when they're ready to be served. The taste is so extraordinary that you won't believe it till you try it. And you don't need a lot of pesto. Even on spaghetti, use just a little.

I've tried this with grouper, cod, haddock, sole, flounder, and once on Spanish mackerel. With these fish it's OK, but nothing to jump up and down about. It's best with the lean white fish.

Beat some pesto into softened butter or margarine. Add just a little at a time tasting as you go. Spread this on fish either before or after cooking.

Another great taste is a little pesto added to a good mayonnaise. Use this for tartar sauce. This combination is best served with fresh, raw vegetables or with cold shrimp.

I grow a few herbs in my flowerbeds at home. Basil happens to be one of my favorites. (The aroma is heavenly). A friend, Helen, stopped by one day and I enticed her to take some basil home with her. About an hour later she brought me back some pesto sauce she had made with my basil. I had a swordfish steak out and the grill was already fired up and I was not about to give up the swordfish, so I decided not to wait till the next day to use the pesto on spaghetti. I mixed it with butter and grilled the swordfish with it, and brushed the steak again when it was done. Fantastic!

Anyway, now what do you think of a pesto sauce in a seafood cookbook?

Light Barbeque Sauce

Makes about ¾ cup

- ¼ cup white corn syrup
- ¼ cup white vinegar
- 2 Tbs. tomato paste, or catsup
- ¼ cup oil
- 2 Tbs. Dijon mustard
- Salt and pepper
- 1 tsp. minced onion and/or 1 minced garlic clove (both optional)

Whisk all these together and brush this on fish over charcoal. You can also add a dash or two of hot sauce.

Ginger Sauce

About 1½-2 cups

- ½ cup catsup
- ½ cup sugar
- 4 Tbs. fresh ginger root, grated
- 3 Tbs. white vinegar
- 3 Tbs. dry sherry
- 3 tsp. cornstarch
- 3 tsp. soy sauce
- 3–5 green onion tops, thinly sliced

Bring all these except the onions to a boil in a heavy saucepan, then stir in the onions. This can be spooned over any kind of fish and baked at 400 degrees.

Sour Cream Sauce

Makes about 2 cups
- 1½ cups sour cream
- 1–2 garlic cloves, finely minced
- ½ cup Parmesan or Romano cheese, freshly grated
- 1 egg, well beaten

Broil fish with this sauce spread over it. Be sure the fish is at least 4 inches away from the heat—the sauce will burn if it's too close. The above ingredients are enough for 2–3 pounds of fish.

Orange-Sour Cream Sauce

Makes about ½ cup
- 5 or more Tbs. toasted sesame seeds
- 1 Tbs. orange marmalade
- 2 Tbs. Dijon mustard
- 2–3 Tbs. sour cream

First, toast the sesame seeds in a dry skillet on medium high heat, shaking the skillet till they're light golden brown. Mix the orange marmalade, mustard, and sour cream, and spread this over the fish to bake at 400 degrees.

When ready to serve, sprinkle it with the toasted sesame seeds.

Savory Anchovy Sauce

Makes about ¾–1 cup

- 10 anchovies (more or less, to your taste)
- 2 egg yolks, room temperature
- 1 small garlic clove
- 2 Tbs. lemon juice
- 8 Tbs. butter, melted and hot
- ½ cup vegetable oil, slightly heated
- 6 large parsley sprigs, without stems
- ¼ tsp. white pepper

Blend the anchovies, egg yolks, and garlic. Blend one tablespoon of lemon juice. Mix the butter and oil together and with the blender running, add a quarter cup of this mixture a drop at a time, then add the rest in a slow steady stream. Don't stop the blender or the stream at any time. Mix the other tablespoon of lemon juice with the parsley and white pepper to taste, just till the parsley is chopped. Add more lemon juice to taste if desired. If the sauce is too thick, blend a little warm water.

This is delicious on broiled or fried fish. It becomes as spreadable as butter in the refrigerator.

Italian-Style Nutty-Cheese Sauce

Enough for 2 lbs. fish

- 1 lb. Ricotta cheese
- 2 eggs lightly beaten
- 2 garlic cloves
- ½ cup Parmesan or Romano cheese, freshly grated
- 1 tsp. each oregano and basil

(continued next page)

> **4 Tbs. melted butter or margarine**
> **½ cup heavy whipping cream**
> **½ cup walnuts, finely chopped**
> **2 Tbs. chopped parsley**
> **Salt and pepper**

Blend the Ricotta cheese, eggs, garlic, Parmesan or Romano cheese, oregano, basil, butter, and cream. Heat this in a saucepan with the nuts and parsley, but don't let it boil. Season it with salt and pepper.

This can be spread on fish before broiling or served separately.

This was one of my recipes when my food-love was Italian. I had originally prepared it to serve on fettucine. Then I decided to try on some Hog-Snapper fillets, and it was delicious.

Italian Herbed-Mayonnaise Sauce

Makes about 2 cups
> **1 cup mayonnaise (*not* salad dressing)**
> **¼ cup white wine vinegar**
> **¼ cup minced parsley**
> **½ cup white wine**
> **1 small medium-size onion**
> **1 Tbs. chopped garlic, packed in oil or**
> **   fresh minced**
> **3 tsp. Italian herbs**
> **Freshly ground pepper or white pepper**

Purée everything except the mayonnaise in a blender, then reduce this to about a half a cup in a medium-size saucepan on medium high heat. Stir in the mayonnaise and heat till it's warm but don't let it boil. If it's too thin don't cook it down, add mayonnaise.

Simply mix the ingredients of the following butter
sauces and pour them over fish for baking.

Lemon, Thyme, And Butter Sauce

Makes about ¾ cup
- ¼   cup lemon juice
- ½   cup melted butter or margarine
- 1   tsp. dried thyme leaves

Lemon, Butter, And Caper Sauce

Makes about ¾ cup
- ¼   cup lemon juice
- ½   cup melted butter
- 2   tsp. capers

Sherried Butter Sauce

Make about ¾ cup
- 1   part melted butter
- 2   parts dry white sherry

Sesame-Ginger Marinade For Grouper
(or any thick fish)

For 2 lbs. fish
- 1 cup fish stock or chicken broth
- ½ cup teriyaki sauce
- ¼ cup honey
- 1–2 tsp. toasted sesame oil
- 1 Tbs. garlic, finely minced
- 1 Tbs. fresh ginger root, finely grated

Heat the fish stock before adding the rest of the ingredients, then cool this mixture to room temperature.

Pour this over the fish in a shallow glass or any non-metallic dish and marinate for 2–4 hours, or even overnight, turning the fish several times. This marinade is enough for about 2-1/2 pounds of fish. And you can refrigerate any leftovers for future use.

I was in a hurry for dinner one night and I wanted to use this recipe, because it's so good! I heated the marinade and added a tablespoon of cornstarch to thicken it a little, put the grouper in a shallow pan, poured the mixture over the fish and broiled it, twice. It was delicious!

Garlic-Dill Marinade for Swordfish

Makes about ¾ cup
- ½ cup vegetable oil
- ¼ cup white wine
- 1 garlic clove, crushed and minced
- 1 Tbs. tomato paste
- 2 Tbs. fresh minced dill
- Salt and white pepper

Mix these ingredients and marinate a pound of swordfish steaks in the mixture for about two hours, turning frequently.

Or it can be refrigerated and allowed to marinate overnight. Ya can also marinate the steaks in a cooking bag—there's no need for turning them, and no odor in your refrigerator!

This is a delicious and simple marinade and can also be used with any lean white fish.

Champagne Batter for Deep-Fried Seafood

Makes enough for 2 lbs. fish

- 1¼ cups all-purpose flour
- 1¼ cup dry champagne
- 2 eggs, separated
- 3 Tbs. butter or margarine, melted and cooled
- Salt and pepper
- Pinch cream of tartar

Put the flour in a large bowl and make a well in the center. Pour in the egg yolks, salt, pepper, and just over half the champagne. Whisk these together, then gradually mix the flour into the liquid to form a smooth paste and gently stir in enough of the remaining champagne to make a thick batter, without over mixing. Let this stand at room temperature for at least an hour.

Then, beat the egg whites with the cream of tartar till this is stiff but not dry. Fold less than half of this into the above batter, then fold the batter into the rest.

The batter is very light and airy. It doesn't overwhelm seafood. And it's excellent with stone-crab claws. Since the meat in a stone crab is already cooked, the batter browns nicely and the crabmeat doesn't get a chance to be cooked again.

But throw out any leftover batter—it's no good once it goes flat.

Beer Batter--Plain and Simple

Makes 2 cups
- 1   cups all-purpose flour
- 1   Tbs. cornstarch
- 1   cup beer

Mix these and add salt and pepper to taste. This is good with any seafood, and especially shrimp, scallops, and fish.

For Shellfish

Teriyaki Sauce for Barbecued Shrimp

Equal amounts of:

Teriyaki sauce
Unsweetened pineapple juice

Then add:

Half the above amount of melted butter or
margarine
Fresh or frozen shrimp, peeled and deveined, with
tails left on

Mix the liquid ingredients in a glass bowl, lay the shrimp in this, and leave it at room temperature for no more than an hour, or in the refrigerator for several hours, stirring often.

Now mix about a tablespoon of cornstarch into the remaining marinade and bring this to a boil, stirring constantly. Use this as an additional dipping sauce.

These shrimp, grilled or broiled, are good as either an appetizer or a main course. You can skewer them to make the turning easier.

Dipping Sauce for Stone-Crab Claws, Shrimp, or Alaskan King Crab

Makes about 1¼ cups
    3 tsp. dry mustard
    1 cup mayonnaise
 2–3 tsp. Pickapeppa sauce
    2 Tbs. heavy cream

Whisk these with a wire whip till the mixture reaches a creamy consistency, adding more cream if it's too thick.

Dilled Sour Cream Sauce

Makes about 1¼ cup

- ⅔ cup mayonnaise (*not* salad dressing)
- ¼ cup sour cream
- 1 tsp. dried dill weed
- 1 Tbs. Romano or Parmesan cheese, freshly grated (but Romano is best)
- 1 Tbs. onion, chopped
- 1 tsp. tarragon vinegar
- 1 tsp. fresh lemon or lime juice
- ½–1 tsp. white pepper
- 2 dashes of Worcestershire sauce
- 1 garlic clove
- Salt

Blend all these and chill for the flavors to blend. This can be served cold with cold cocktail shrimp, as a topping for cold salmon, or with smoked fish of any kind.

For Pasta

Basic Marinara Sauce

About 3 cups
- ½ cup olive oil
- 3 fresh garlic cloves, pressed
- 1 Tbs. dried whole oregano, or 2 Tbs. fresh minced
- 1 Tbs. dried parsley leaves, or 2 Tbs. fresh minced
- 1 large can Italian tomatoes, packed in tomato juice or sauce
- Salt and pepper

Heat the olive oil, garlic, oregano, and parsley in a medium-size saucepan on medium heat. Add salt and pepper and cook this for 2–3 minutes while stirring.

Now add the tomatoes. Squeeze each tomato through your fingers. This doesn't crush it completely, but reduces the bulk. (The Italian-style [Pomodori] tomatoes don't have many seeds.) Add the liquid from the can and cook this on medium heat for 15–20 minutes.

Add two tablespoons of tomato paste first if the tomatoes are packed in juice.

The Marinara can be served on spaghetti or linguine and on seafood—this is the basic sauce for several of the recipes in this book.

Squid-Marinara Sauce

Makes about 2½ cups

- 2 cups basic marinara sauce
- 1 lb. frozen squid, already cleaned, ready to thaw and use

When the squid is thawed, cut the body crosswise, making rings from the cuts. Turn each of the rings inside out, rinse and pat them dry. Use the tentacles too, if they're included.

Heat the sauce, add the squid rings and tentacles, and cook this just till the squid turns creamy white and loses its transparency. Do *not* overcook these. You don't want to think you are eating rubber bands!

Sherried Seafood-Cream Sauce

Makes about 2½ cups

- ½ cup pine (pignoli) nuts
- 3 Tbs. butter or margarine
- 3 Tbs. all-purpose flour
- 1 cup half-and-half
- ½ cup chicken broth
- ¼ cup dry sherry
- 3 Tbs. dehydrated parsley, or fresh minced
- Salt and white pepper
- ½–1 lb. shellfish (shrimp, lobster, clams, king crab leg meat, stone-crab claw meat, blue-crab meat, rock shrimp, or any combination you like)

Toast the pine nuts in a pie plate at 350 degrees till they're light brown.

Melt the butter in a saucepan and cook the flour while stirring for a couple of minutes. Slowly add the half-and-half and the chicken broth while stirring; when this has come to a boil stir in the rest of the ingredients and heat it again, but don't let it boil.

This sauce is excellent on any seafood and over any type of pasta. It's also great on the puff pastries that you get in the freezer section of your supermarket.

Sometimes I add a little chopped pimiento for color.

White Clam Sauce

Makes about 1½ cups

 3 Tbs. olive oil
 2 large garlic cloves, minced, or 1 Tbs. prepared
   minced garlic
 ½ tsp. oregano leaves
 1 Tbs. cornstarch
 The liquor drained from clams with water or bottled
   clam juice added to make 1½ cups
one 10-oz. can whole baby clams, drained
 1 Tbs. parsley, minced
 Salt and freshly ground black pepper

Cook the olive oil, garlic, and oregano in a small, heavy saucepan for about 3 minutes.

Mix the cornstarch and the clam broth, add this to the saucepan and cook without boiling till it's slightly thickened. Add the clams and just heat through.

Serve over shells or linguine and sprinkle with minced parsley.

You can also use fresh, steamed clams and bottled clam juice for variation. And if you don't like a real clammy taste, use water instead of clam juice.

The following all make enough for 1–1-1/2 lbs. of spaghetti.

Red Clam Sauce

- ¼ **cup red or rosé wine**
- ¼ **cup clam juice (from the canned baby clams)**
- 2 **cups basic marinara sauce**
- 1 **can whole baby clams**

Heat the wine and clam juice in a medium-size saucepan till reduced to half. Add 2 cups of marinara sauce and heat this just to boiling, before adding the clams. Heat this just till the clams are hot but don't let it boil.

Serve this over linguine, spaghetti, or shells. There are some baby shells on the market made with semolina flour, that are much better than the regular macaroni shells.

Red Shrimp Sauce

- 2 **cups basic marinara sauce**
- 1 **lb. small or medium shrimp, peeled and deveined**

Heat the sauce in a medium-size saucepan add the shrimp and continue to cook them on medium heat till they turn pink on the outside and opaque.

Serve this over linguine or spaghetti.

Red Lobster Sauce

- 2 **cups basic marinara sauce**
- 2 **Tbs. sherry**
- 1 **lb. lobster meat, uncooked**

Heat the sauce with the sherry till it's bubbly, add the lobster, cut into cubes or medallions, and cook this just till the lobster turns opaque.

Dips
and
Spreads

Special Shrimp-and-Cheese Dip

Makes about 4 cups

- 1 lb. cooked shrimp, peeled, deveined, and finely chopped
- 1 lb. Ricotta cheese
- ½ lb. cream cheese, room temperature
- ½ lb. bleu cheese, crumbled
- 1 stick butter, melted but not hot
- 3 Tbs. chicken base, dry or creamy but not cubes
- 2 tsp. sweet paprika (preferably Hungarian if available)

Mix the cheeses together. Blend the butter, chicken base, paprika, and shrimp in another bowl. Stir in the cheese mixture till it's thoroughly blended, and refrigerate this in a serving bowl. Serve it with crackers and crudites.

Small-curd cottage cheese (not creamy style) can be substituted for the Ricotta. And regular paprika can be used instead of the sweet—it's a lot cheaper.

Shrimp-and-Artichoke Dip

Makes about 2½ cups

- ¼–½ lb. cooked shrimp
- 1–2 tsp. onion, finely minced
- 1 cup sour cream
- 1 jar marinated artichokes, *not* drained
- Salt and white pepper

Purée the shrimp in a blender, then add the onion, sour cream, artichokes, and the oil they are packed in, and blend these till they're smooth and creamy. Add salt and pepper to taste and chill this for at least 2 hours.

I've also used this dip as a sauce to pass with baked or broiled fish. I'm a great artichoke lover. I think you'll find this the greatest taste combination ever. You can also substitute crabmeat for the shrimp. But, of course, you don't purée the crabmeat, just pick it over well and shred it.

Hot Crab Dip

Makes about 3 cups

8-oz. pkg. cream cheese, softened
   3 Tbs. lemon or lime juice
   2 Tbs. ranch-style, dry salad dressing
   3 Tbs. mayonnaise (*not* salad dressing)
  ¼ cup pimiento-stuffed olives, minced
  ½ lb. crabmeat, fresh, canned, or frozen
       and thawed
 Salt and white pepper
Dash hot sauce (optional)

Mix the cream cheese, lemon juice, salad dressing, and mayonnaise, then blend in the rest and add salt and pepper to taste.

Bake this till it's heated through at 350 degrees in a buttered baking dish, and garnish it with paprika and lemon slices.

Serve this with crackers of any kind or crunchy bread cubes, or even some vegetables for dipping.

This is a dip that will be gone first, so you might as well make two just in case.

Clam Dip

Makes about 2 cups
- 1 cup fresh clams, steamed, and minced (or canned and well drained)
- ½ cup butter or margarine, softened
- ¼ cup heavy whipping cream
- ½ small onion
- 2 tsp. dehydrated parsley, or 1 Tbs. fresh
- 2 Tbs. pimiento, well-drained
- Salt and pepper

Blend these at a medium speed till they're smooth and creamy. Refrigerate this in a buttered bowl covered tightly with plastic wrap, and take it out about half an hour before serving.

Serve it on crackers and garnish it with pimiento and lemon slices.

Spreads

Shrimp Spread

Makes about 2½ cups
- 12 oz. cream cheese, softened
- 2 Tbs. Worcestershire sauce
- 2 Tbs. fresh lemon juice
- 1 Tbs. butter
- 1 small onion, minced
- Sprinkle of dill weed

Mix these together and work the mixture into a round shape of about an inch thick on a serving platter. Spread a half bottle of chili sauce over this to the thickness of pizza sauce and sprinkle a cup (or 8-oz. can) of small boiled shrimp, or crabmeat, on top. Serve them with crackers.

Shrimp, Cheese, and Anchovy Spread

Makes about 3½ cups
- 8 oz. cream cheese
- 4 anchovies, rinsed and patted dry
- 3 Tbs. butter or margarine
- 1 Tbs. lemon juice
- 2 tsp. Dijon mustard
- 1 lb. cooked shrimp, peeled, deveined, and cold
- 1 large green onion, sliced and chopped
- 1 Tbs. capers, rinsed and patted dry
- Salt and pepper

Blend the cream cheese, anchovies, butter, lemon juice, and mustard till they're smooth. Add the shrimp and chop them finely. Scrape this mixture into a medium-size bowl, blend in the green onion, capers, salt, and pepper, and press this into a buttered or oiled form or bowl. Refrigerate this covered for at least 8 hours.

Serve this on a bed of lettuce with crackers or cocktail rye bread. Let it stand at room temperature for at least an hour before serving.

If you would like a milder anchovy flavor, soak them in milk for about 10 minutes, then rinse and pat them dry. I would rather do this than use fewer anchovies, because the flavor is much better.

I like to top this spread with a thin layer of a little sour cream mixed with a small cucumber (peeled, seeded, salted, and chopped). If you don't want to spraed this over your beautiful mold, you can serve it on the side, a dollop for each cracker with spread.

Shrimpy Cream-Cheese Spread

Makes about 1 qt. bowl

   ½ lb. cooked shrimp, peeled, deveined, and
      finely chopped
one 8-oz. pkg. cream cheese
   ½ cup slivered almonds, chopped and toasted
   ½ cup crushed pineapple, well-drained
   ¼ cup ripe olives, finely chopped
   1 Tbs. lemon juice

Mix all these and refrigerate for about an hour. Take it out about an hour before serving.

Use this as a spread for crackers. I make it for spreading on slices of cocktail rye bread, for hors d'oeuvres. Cut diagonally, they make great finger food.

Shrimp Paté

Makes about 3 cups

   1 lb. shrimp, peeled and deveined
   2 Tbs. butter or margarine
   1 Tbs. hot mustard, or Dijon
   2 Tbs. sherry
1 to 2 Tbs. lemon juice
   8 Tbs. melted butter or margarine
   2 Tbs. pimiento, patted dry and chopped
   1 Tbs. freeze-dried chives

Sauté the shrimp in two tablespoons of butter, without over-cooking them. Blend the shrimp, mustard, sherry, and lemon juice till the shrimp are finely chopped. You'll have to remove the lid often to push the mixture into the blades. (Be sure to turn the blender off and wait till the blades stop turning).

Now pour in the melted 8 tablespoons of butter and blend this till it's well mixed, then stir in the pimiento and chives.

Gently press the mixture into a greased form pan and chill it overnight, or make it in the morning and allow it to chill all day. The flavors have a chance to mellow if they're left for 24 hours, but it can be served after 4 hours. Serve it with crackers, cocktail rye bread, or Melba toast. You'll need a 3-cup-size form, or dish or pan. And you can use butter, oil, or mayonnaise to coat it with.

Crabmeat Paté

Use 3—4 cup mold
- two 8-oz. pkgs. cream cheese, softened
- ½ lb. crabmeat
- 1 Tbs. dry sherry
- 2 Tbs. fish bouillon (made from cubes) or cream heavy or light
- Salt and white pepper
- Dash or two Worcestershire sauce

Mix the cream cheese and crabmeat, and gently add the sherry and seasonings and whatever liquid you choose— using more liquid to thin as necessary.

Spread a thin layer of mayonnaise, butter, or oil in a mold or bowl and chill this either overnight or for at least 4 hours. Serve it with crackers or a cocktail rye.

Usually your seafood market will carry a very good fish bouillon cube. Use it double strength for this recipe.

Sometimes I use shrimp or lobster instead of crabmeat. The flavor is great. They should be cooked and puréed first, and I use cream or half-and-half with them, not bouillon.

Cheesy Crab Log

12 ounces cream cheese, softened
½ lb. crabmeat
2 Tbs. butter or margarine, room temperature
2 Tbs. fresh onion, finely minced
1 tsp. lemon juice
1 Tbs. Worcestershire sauce
2 Tbs. minced pimiento
½ cup nuts--pecans, walnuts, or peanuts, finely chopped

Mix all these except the nuts and form into one or two logs by rolling them inside a sheet of wax paper. Chill these till they're firm, then roll them in the nuts. You don't have to be choosy about the kinds of nuts. I use whatever I have on hand. I've even used pine nuts. These are quite expensive but sure are good with this combination of cheese and crab.

These crab logs can be served at room temperature or directly from the refrigerator. If they're cold you'll need spreaders.

Mayonnaise

Makes about 2½ cups
1 egg, room temperature
4 tsp. lemon juice
2 tsp. Dijon mustard with seeds
½ tsp. white pepper
1–2 dashes hot sauce
Salt
1½ cup safflower oil
½ cup virgin olive oil

Blend the egg, lemon juice, mustard, pepper, hot sauce, and salt. With the blender running, slowly add the safflower and olive oils through the small opening on top. This will keep in the refrigerator for about 5 days.

This mayonnaise is excellent with fish as is or with different herbs to suit the occasion, for instance, dill weed with salmon. It's also good on a tossed salad or a dish of sliced tomatoes.

Onion Mayonnaise

Makes about 1¼ cups

>   2   medium-size mild onions, quartered
>   1   cup mayonnaise
>   1   Tbs. dry sherry

Purée the onions in a blender, then stir them into the mayonnaise, add the sherry, and mix this well.

Use this with fried or broiled fish instead of regular tartar sauce, or as a dip for shrimp.

Sesame-Seed Paste (Tahini) with Yogurt

Makes about 2¾ cups

>   ½   cup Tahini
>   2   cups plain yogurt
>   2–3   garlic cloves, or to taste
>   2   Tbs. dried parsley
>   1–2   Tbs. lemon juice

Blend the Tahini, yogurt, garlic, and parsley till they're smooth. Add the lemon juice a little bit at a time, and chill this till you're ready to use it.

This is great on baked or broiled fish.

Butters

Shrimp Butter

Makes about 2 cups
- 1½ tsp. dried dill weed
- 3 small shallots
- 10 medium shrimp, cooked
- 1 stick of unsalted butter, well chilled and cut into tablespoon-size pieces
- 1½ Tbs. fresh lemon juice
- 1½ tsp. Pickapeppa sauce

Chop the dill weed and shallots in a blender, using the on-and-off button, for about 15 seconds. Blend in the shrimp till they're coarsely chopped. Add the butter one piece at a time. In between pieces of butter add drops of lemon juice and Pickapeppa sauce. You may have to stop the blender occasionally to push the mixture down into the blades. You can add salt to taste if you like.

The ways to use your shrimp butter are endless.

TRY THIS:

Broil or bake fish fillets for a few minutes without adding anything, then spread the shrimp butter all over them and finish cooking them.Spread them again with the shrimp butter and garnish them with lemon and parsley. Toasted sesame seeds make a nice topping on the shrimp butter, too.

AND:

Soften an 8-ounce package of cream cheese and whip it with about a tablespoon of cream. Mix in the shrimp butter (room temperature), press this mixture into an oiled mold and chill it. Serve it on a bed of lettuce with garnish of your choice and with different kinds of crackers and crudites.

AND:

Thin the shrimp butter with a litle more lemon juice, enough so you can blend it into sour cream. Serve this in a bowl with chips, pretzels, bread sticks, crackers, or fresh vegetable sticks. Excellent!

Nutty Browned Butter

Makes about ½ cup

1 **stick butter or margarine**
¼ **cup pecans, sesame seeds*, or sunflower seeds**, finely minced**

Cook the butter while stirring on medium-high heat till all the milk solids have evaporated. It will start to brown very quickly thus so watch it closely. Stir in the nuts and spoon this over fish to serve immediately.

*Toast the sesame seeds in a skillet, shaking the skillet till the seeds brown very lightly.

**Buy the roasted variety or toast them the same as sesame seeds.

Macadamia-Nut Butter

Makes about ¾ cup

4 **Tbs. butter or margarine, room temperature**
½ **cup Macadamia nuts**
Fresh lemon

Grind the nuts in the blender and mix them into the butter with just a squeeze or two of fresh lemon juice.

Spread this over cooked fish.

SIMPLY MIX THE INGREDIENTS IN THE FOLLOWING:

EACH MAKES ABOUT ½–¾ CUPS

MUSTARD BUTTER

- ½ cup butter
- ¼ cup Dijon mustard
- 2 Tbs. freeze-dried chives

ORANGE-MUSTARD BUTTER

- ½ cup butter
- ¼ cup Dijon mustard
- 1 Tbs. orange zest: just the very orange part of the skin

GARLIC BUTTER

- ½ cup butter
- 3 large garlic cloves, minced
- 1 Tbs. fresh parsley, finely minced

GARLIC-CHEESE BUTTER

- ½ cup butter
- 3 medium-size garlic cloves
- 2 Tbs. Parmesan cheese

BLEU-CHEESE BUTTER

- ½ cup butter
- ¼ cup crumbled bleu cheese

FRESH BASIL BUTTER

- ½ cup butter
- ¼ cup fresh basil leaves, minced

TARRAGON-LEMON BUTTER

- ½ cup butter
- 1 Tbs. fresh tarragon or 1 tsp. dried tarragon
- 2 tsp. lemon juice

HERB BUTTER

- ½ cup butter
- 1 tsp. mixed herbs
- 1 tsp. lemon juice

VINEGAR BUTTER

- ½ cup butter
- 2 Tbs. cider vinegar
- 1 Tbs. dehydrated parsley

DILLED BUTTER

- ½ cup butter
- 2 Tbs. fresh dill, minced or 1 Tbs. dried dill weed